Golden Opportunities

A Biographical History of Montana's Jewish Communities

by
Julie L. Coleman

Library of Congress Catalog Card Number: 94-71891

ISBN: 1-56044-298-0

Published by Julie L. Coleman, P. O. Box 21904
Billings, Montana 59104, in cooperation with
SkyHouse Publishers, an imprint of Falcon Press™, Helena, Montana.

Design, typesetting, and other prepress work by SkyHouse Publishers.

Distributed by Falcon Press™. To order, write to P. O. Box 1718,
Helena, Montana 59624, or call 1-800-582-2665.

First Edition

Manufactured in the United States of America.

This book is dedicated to the memory of my parents, William B. and Esther H. Levy, who instilled in me the love for and dedication to my family, my Jewish heritage, and learning, and to my granddaughters, Linday Blair and Lauren Jo Brown, whom I hope will continue these ideals.

Contents

FOREWORD

Jews have had a long association with Montana: they were among the earliest settlers in and, indeed, founders of many of Montana's towns and cities. Yet the Jewish population of the state has always been small. Today, Jews number less than one-tenth of one percent of the state's population. Moreover, it has never been easy to maintain Jewish communal life in Montana, where Jewish books are, at times, more difficult to obtain than bagels! Given the small Jewish population, why then a history of the Jewish communities of Montana? Who will be interested?

Golden Opportunities is, first and foremost, a book that will interest historians and those interested in history. In many ways, Montana is a challenge to the historian. It is marked by contradictions and often defies easy explanations. Montana is a place of grand yet fragile beauty, sculpted by God and the glaciers, adorned by nature, too often scarred by greed. Traders and trappers, miners and industrialists, railroad tycoons and absentee landowners have always shared this corner of America with men, women, and families seeking only home and sustenance. For the most part, they have struggled successfully to live and work together. Sometimes there have been conflicts. Julie Coleman describes those conflicts and struggles reflected in the lives of some Montana citizens who felt them the most. The histories recounted in this book rely heavily on eyewitness accounts and personal recollections, the grist for every good historian's mill.

Others outside the trade of history will also find this book fascinating reading. It tells a marvelous tale of survival, a tale as old as the Jewish people. Why would Jews leave the familiar comforts of St. Louis or Cinncinnati, New York or Chicago, to move to the Montana frontier? Why did Jews stay, faced often with hardship and isolation? Why, when unity and conformity would seem to ensure a community, was the Jewish experience in Montana so often marked by diversity, even dissension? And how can we explain the fact that the Jewish communities of Montana have survived and are viable to this day, even by some standards thriving?

Although separated by time and distance, the Jewish experience in Montana is remarkably similar to the Jewish experience in ancient Israel, fifth-century Babylonia, fourteenth-century Spain, or nineteenth-century Russia. As we understand why and how Jews have survived in Montana, we have a better understanding of why and how Jews survived in other places and at other times.

There is also a prescriptive reason to read this book, and to learn about this people and these communities: it will teach us all to appreciate our similarities, and to respect our differences. Montana comprises citizens of many races, religions, and ethnic or national backgrounds. It has always been, and will continue to be, a challenge for this diverse population—Jews and gentiles, immigrants and Native Americans, whites and peoples of color—to live and work together as neighbors. If the state and its citizens are to prosper, particularly in this time when differences among peoples are suspect, they must meet the challenge.

The *Mishna*, an ancient book of Jewish lore, contains the following maxim: "Who is wise? The one who learns from all people." This book will help us learn from some of Montana's people, a people small in numbers but rich in experience. It is a good place to start on the road to wisdom.

RABBI KENNETH E. EHRLICH
Dean, Hebrew Union College—
Jewish Institute of Religion
Cinncinnati, Ohio,
and former
Rabbi, Congregation Beth Aaron,
Billings, Montana,
(1983-1985)

Introduction

In May of 1952, I moved to Billings, Montana, from Chicago, Illinois. Our family of four—my lawyer husband, Melvin A. Brown, and my two small children, Barbara and Richard, and I—were all Chicago-born and raised in a predominantly Jewish neighborhood. Mel had been a navigator in World War II and had been a German prisoner of war; I had been at the University of Wisconsin during that time, and I suppose we were "the new generation" of the era.

For us and our families, our moving to Montana was akin to the early pioneers leaving their families to try new lands and new experiences. In fact, when we were settled and my parents came to visit, they hired a photographer to take pictures of our home and the surrounding area so that they could show the relatives and friends in Chicago we were actually living in a civilized place!

Mel, who worked for my uncle in Chicago, came to develop an investment business in the oil industry. At the time, Billings was fast becoming a boom town. The development of the Williston basin attracted major oil companies who located in the largest city of eastern Montana, and also beckoned lawyers, geologists, land men, drillers—anyone who smelled economic opportunity from the "black gold." In such an atmosphere, we felt we were modern day pioneers. We were "big city people." As far as we could tell, we were the only Jews connected with the mushrooming oil business that used Billings as its center; it was new for us to be moving into a predominantly non-Jewish environment.

We soon discovered that there was a Jewish congregation in Billings, and that there were a number of young Jewish couples with small children who had moved here in recent years. Although there was a smattering of professionals, most of the Billings Jews were in the retail business. Most of the newcomers were college educated, in contrast to the older generation who had been in Montana for many years. Because we newcomers came from areas that had long-established Jewish congregations we brought ideas from a number of backgrounds. We formed a diverse congregation that had to compromise on ritual.

Since we younger members of the congregation were all parents of the postwar "baby boomers," the first thing we emphasized was Sunday School. We all found ourselves teaching classes that filled with our growing numbers of children. Our social activities centered on the Temple, too, and we had many parties, dances, and even hired dance instructors to teach us the new dance steps.

Searching for more links to our community, we discovered that Billings had a history of Jewish organizations. Jewish women had formed a Ladies Aid Society in 1915; in 1917, when the B'nai B'rith lodge was organized, the women petitioned to become a B'nai B'rith auxiliary. By 1918 a Jewish cemetery was dedicated on Broadwater Avenue, and a congregation was formed to support it. I had been in Billings just two years when, in 1954, a Temple sisterhood was formed as an arm of the congregation, and in an effort to work with the broader community the women joined the city's Federation of Women's Clubs, which had representation from such diverse areas as the Phyllis Wheatley Club (a black women's organization), the Junior Women's Club, and the Women's Christian Temperance Society. I was sent as a delegate from Temple Beth Aaron, and within a year, I found myself president of the Federation. This began a long history of volunteer work for me.

The early 1950s also saw the beginning of the Billings chapter of the League of Women Voters. This organization proved to be a magnet for women like me—college educated, not working, raising small children, and starved for adult conversation and some feeling of individual accomplishment. The women who worked together at this time formed the nucleus of life-long friendships. Membership in the League unexpectedly led me into research for this book. After serving as president of the Billings organization, I was elected to the state board, which necessitated frequent trips to Helena. There I met Frieda Fligelman, a League member and the daughter of one of Helena's early Jewish merchants. Frieda filled me with tales of early Helena. She took me to the Jewish cemetery there and to the homes of elderly Jewish women who were eager to talk about the past. I was amazed to learn that Jews had been in Montana during the gold rush days, and that there had been Jewish miners, adventurers, and participants in early Montana government. Until I met Frieda I had shared a common misperception about Jewish immigrants, assuming that most Jews had settled in the large eastern cities and had lived in self-imposed ghettos among their fellow countrymen. When I learned about the young Jewish miners and entrepreneurs who had struggled west, I was convinced that someone should get the experiences of these elderly children of pioneers in print before the original sources were gone.

So, armed with a reel-to-reel tape recorder, I went back to Helena and began to tape personal interviews. I learned that minutes of the United Hebrew Benevolent Association were in the vault at Helena's Union Bank and Trust Company, and I received permission to read them and take notes. The minutes are now kept at the Montana Historical Society. The people in Helena with whom I spoke were enthusiastic about my project, and they suggested that I go to Butte and interview people there. I contacted several Butte Jews, received a gracious response, and my first visit was at a dinner arranged for me so that I could meet a number of longtime Butte residents and their children. I visited their places of business, copied their congregation records, and came back to Billings and transcribed the taped interviews.

Library work followed this, and because I was on the Billings Library Board by that time, I knew about interlibrary loans, and the librarian was most helpful in aiding me with available resource material. I pored through many old books looking for Jewish-sounding names. I also began to read anything I could find on Montana history. I picked up little bits of information from many sources. If there are discrepancies in spelling or names in this book, it is because of the varied and often contradictory source material. I found that often men were identified only by first initial and last name, for instance, so spent much time finding first names. Women often were called by nicknames that had little to do with their given names. In several cases what sounded like two different people turned out to be one person. Since much of my research was done in the 1960s, the only scholarly material available was one master's thesis written about Montana Jews by Rabbi Benjamin Kelson, presented to the University of Montana in 1950. Kelson was a Reform rabbi in Butte when he did his research, and when I interviewed Butte Jews some fifteen years after his thesis was prepared, many were not complimentary about the accuracy of his work. After reading my chapter on Butte, this may become more understandable. There were three congregations in that chaotic city, with much acrimony between them. Since Rabbi Kelson was Reform, the Orthodox, and the Conservative Jews did not feel that he had explored all of their history adequately.

As I read Kelson's thesis originally, then reread it in 1993, I wondered why he dismissed Billings as he did. He stated that no community life emerged and that "no records of achievement or uniqueness" existed, suggesting no history of Billings Jews could be written. Other sources expressed similar dismay at the lack of material, and seem ready to make quick decisions about the Billings Jews. More recently, articles about Montana Jewry have appeared in such national press as the *New York Times*, July 26, 1993, which stated that "Congregations have formed in more cosmopolitan Billings and Missoula, but their meeting places are informal." I had, by that time, learned a great deal about Billings Jewish history, which stretched back to the beginning of the century. Billings has had a Jewish cemetery from 1918 and a temple building since 1940. It had the same full-time rabbi from 1954 to 1980 and two full-time rabbis and regularly visiting student rabbis since, so inaccuracies in the press and other sources abound.

When the *New York Times* article appeared, I was inundated with copies of the article and requests to "set the record straight." I dug out the research I had done and determined that it be made available through print. Originally, my efforts focused on Helena and Butte because they were the earliest Jewish communities. However, since Billings probably has the largest Jewish community now, and since I have access to much original source material, I hope to feature it most strongly, and accomplish two other things through this book.

First, I would like to dispel the commonly held notion (by Jews and non-Jews alike) that all the immigrant Jews of the mid-1800s came from the old world, settled in the large cities and worked at whatever job they could find (mainly in the garment industry or the fur industry because that is what they had learned in Europe) and stayed there. Many did, of course, but there were also adventurers, very young men and women who for the most part were looking for riches, excitement, and new opportunities; Montana attracted them. They were usually young, German men, most still in their teens, who were willing to undertake the dangerous trek west to search out their fortunes. For most, the journey to Montana Territory was extremely difficult. Some travelled the overland trail from Salt Lake City; others got to Denver and then came across the plains via the Lander Cut-off and Soda Springs to Virginia City; some used the stagecoach; others came through Canada to Vancouver and backtracked to Montana; and still others crossed the Isthmus of Panama or came from the California gold fields looking for new opportunities. No matter which direction the newcomers came from, their journey was fraught with danger. I hope to show how they made it to Montana and formed the roots of Judaism in the state.

Second, by focusing on the three major cities and using much of the biographical material I gleaned from the interviews and research, I would like to go beyond the commonly known historical facts and present some of the people who were active in their communities. As I interviewed people, I asked about their childhoods and their entries into the workforce. I wanted a picture of what Jewish life in Montana was like and wanted to see if it differed from that of more established cities and states. I present material on Billings that seems to be lacking in any of the available research materials. As I have perused Billings sources, I have found a wealth of original material—from early checking accounts to business records, organizational minutes, pictures, and interviews.

I realize that my research method, by the nature of the approach, overlooks many people who were not mentioned in the various texts I used or were not among the people I interviewed, but I hope that the sampling is broad enough to show how different each of the three Jewish communities were, and also what they had in common.

Commonalities abound. The need to bury the dead in a traditional manner is the most common thread running among the three communities I studied. The Jews in each of these small cities had to organize a burial society and to establish a cemetery; in each case this led to the beginnings of one or more congregations for worship. The congregations then grew as families did: intense family loyalty resulted in brothers sending for brothers, uncles sending for nephews, relatives sending to Europe for relatives left behind, and thus expanding the members of the Temple. The tradition of marrying within the faith resulted in arranged marriages, relatives marrying relatives, and men traveling to larger cities to look for Jewish brides to bring back west. Although the earliest arrivals to Virginia City and the gold fields were single, as they settled down, most managed to find Jewish wives, and Jewish women became a part of the history. Often sisters in one family married brothers of another family, or the children of one family grew up to marry the children of friends, connecting the community.

Not all Jewish lives in Montana were defined by traditional family values. There were, of course, some Jewish women who were desperate to earn a living or forced for other reasons to turn to the oldest profession, or who were brought west for that expressed purpose, and the stories of the earlier settlements (Butte, particularly) mention some of them by name. I have not found evidence of Jewish prostitutes in Billings, but that may be because they did not merit any particular notice; Billings old-timers assured me there were no Jewish prostitutes in the city, but not everyone identified herself by religious background. I had a similar response in Helena. However, the stories about several "ladies of the night" from Butte have been passed around and provide some flavor of the times of that raucous mining town.

There were more visible common threads between the three communities. B'nai B'rith, the Jewish lodge organization, was also a part of each Montana Jewish community. The Masonic order also attracted Jewish members. Education was another common factor, one that ironically caused each of the Montana towns, in turn, to lose much of their Jewish population. The urge to educate children and to have them meet other Jewish people of their age resulted in many younger Jews going out of state for educations, then not returning to Montana. This pattern is still lamented today.

The differences between the three Montana communities I studied were numerous. Helena, the first Montana Jewish community, was peopled mainly by German immigrants. Since Jews of Russian descent and Jews of German descent had little in common (as is apparent in any study of European history), it is not surprising Helena hired a Reform Jewish rabbi who had a German background similar to many of those Jews in Helena. The Helena people followed his lead in voting for a Reform congregation, allowing men to leave their heads uncovered during worship and letting men and women sit together. Although a very small cadre of Orthodox Jews was present (a few of the elderly), the Helena congregation was thoroughly German, and never saw the schism in the Jewish population that there was in other cities. The interviewees I spoke to in Helena asserted there was little religious prejudice in their town. Jewish business people joined in community organizations such as the Chamber of Commerce and the Republican and Democratic parties, and served on various boards and commissions. Children played with children of other faiths and went to religious services at friends' places of worship. Newspaper articles about religious events appeared frequently, and Jewish ceremonies, from weddings to the dedication of the Temple, attracted prominent non-Jewish guests.

Butte differed in tone. As a hardrock, copper-mining town, Butte attracted a different mix of Jews. Immigrants came from all nations to work in the mines or work as peddlers who supplied the miners; they eventually established businesses ranging from clothing stores to tobacco stores to saloons to houses of prostitution and gambling. The diverse

European origins of Butte Jews resulted in a diversity of religious practices, and, until dwindling numbers of members forced a compromise in order to keep at least one congregation alive, there were three separate Jewish congregations in Butte: Orthodox, Conservative, and Reform. Butte was such a mixture of religions, educational backgrounds, and national origins that not much prejudice was exhibited there either, or at least the people growing up during the early part of the century did not recall any unpleasantness based on religion. Fights occurred, but they might have been among Jews of different backgrounds as well as with non-Jews. Religion did not seem to be a factor.

Billings was the last of the cities to develop a Jewish community, and it differed from both Helena and Butte. The early Billings Jews came on trains and were almost all peddlers or hide and fur dealers. They entered an established white Protestant city and did not mix with the general populace. Few of them were related to one another, as Jews in the other camps had been. In Billings, the Jews were also, to a man, desperately poor; they struggled to make a living in the few occupations they knew, which resulted in keen competition against each other. Animosities grew from business competition, even though they depended on one another socially. Most of these ambitious Billings entrepreneurs worked six days a week, from morning to late evening, leaving little time for religious observance or civic involvement. When a community eventually grew from their labors, it struggled to find its heritage. The isolation may explain, in part, the response I got when I interviewed Billings residents about prejudice. These twentieth-century pioneers recalled the power of the Ku Klux Klan, the hate group that aimed venom at both Jews and Catholics, in the 1920s. The Billings Klan organized boycotts of Jewish businesses and infiltrated the Masonic order, which had previously been one of the first civic organizations that Jews joined, but for about ten years thereafter did not admit any Jews. There was covert discrimination also. The Hilands Golf Club did not admit Jewish members, and years later, when the Junior League was formed in Billings, I was told by close friends who were in the league how sorry they were I could not join because of my religion; they laid blame on the national organization. Within ten years that policy changed, and younger Jewish women were invited to join.

My personal history is just the latest link in a long chain of Montana Jews. I hope that this study of some of the Jews in Montana cities will encourage others to find their places in Montana's Jewish past, present, and future.

CHAPTER ONE

HELENA

Like other settlers on the Montana frontier, the first Jewish residents of the region followed the gold rush. Gold was discovered in Montana (at Gold Creek, then Bannack) in the 1860s. Miners looking for the shiny metal caused a rush to the wide-open territory. In its boom days, Helena was said to have more millionaires per capita than any other city in the world. With such wealth, the mining camp-turned-city was soon named Montana's capital. It was also home to the first synagogue in the state, and it was there that Montana's first organized Jewish community evolved.

Young Jewish immigrants had found their way to earlier camps on the Montana frontier. At least one, Ben Ezekiel of Virginia City, joined the infamous Montana Vigilantes who took justice into their own hands to bring some semblance of law to an area plagued by a crime ring—a group of bandits run by a sheriff. Another Jewish miner, Lewis Hershfield, realized there was an opportunity to start a bank in the new territory, since Sheriff Henry Plummer's gang was plundering stagecoaches and miners were afraid to send money out. Other Jewish pioneers took their own stakes of gold dust and used them to buy supplies to sell to the miners. These small businessmen grew into a merchant class. On July 26, 1884, when a call was issued that was meant to gather those eligible for a pioneer's organization, the date by which one had to have arrived in Montana for recognition as a Montana pioneer was set at May 26, 1864. The list of those eligible included eleven Jews. Eight of the listed pioneers had become Helena residents.

Helena was the first place these individuals pulled together into a Jewish community. As Helena grew and outsized earlier Montana gold camps, a number of Jewish miners moved to the booming town and established roots there. As a group, Jews were distinctive because they controlled a large part of the retail trade: they distributed all kinds of supplies, food, clothing, and mining equipment to the miners, and they provided banking services by exchanging gold dust for cash and extending credit to other businesses. Their influence was an important link in Helena's transition from a gold camp to a city. They opened businesses ranging from hotels to clothing stores to restaurants, and later branched out into ranching, an occupation forbidden to Jews in Europe.

Many were successful, for varying reasons. Some of the Jews had learned their trade in Europe; others had come to the United States and spent some time with a relative and learned a special skill. Others came and grabbed at available opportunities. Family ties provided a network of connections all over the country, and as businesses grew, and more capital was needed, they often drew upon family resources elsewhere. European history had taught Jews to network with their co-religionists and also to use marital ties to economic advantage. By 1867, the Helena City Directory listed seventeen Jewish dry goods and clothing merchants and three non-Jews in the same businesses. At least four of the seventeen and one of the three tobacco stores were owned jointly by family members.

Generally, the Jewish merchants who settled in Helena during the gold rush days were influential in the business life of the Territory. They had an interest in the future of the community and worked to promote cultural activities. Many became patrons of the arts. Many insisted on their children having music and elocution lessons, which led to performances. Their names are listed in the roster of the Chamber of Commerce, in special event programs, and in various newspaper articles.

Helena's Jewish merchants were necessarily active in local business organizations. In November of 1877, when sixty-three men formed the Helena Board of Trade (a forerunner of the Chamber of Commerce), twelve of its original members were Jews: Abram Sands, Moses Morris, David Goldberg, Henry Klein, Jacob Feldberg, Isaac Greenhood, Jacob Loeb, William J. Auerbach, Venzel C. Rinda, Max Sklower, Edward Zimmerman, and David Morris. Jews also became active in Montana politics, since as early as the 1860s Jacob Feldberg had been on the Virginia City city council. Rather than supporting one party, Jewish political activists supported both and a variety of platforms, professing to be more interested in good government than backing a particular cause.

The Helena Jews were acutely aware of their religious heritage and considered themselves Jewish even though they had no synagogue or rabbi available for services. The need for a properly consecrated burial ground led, in 1866, to the establishment of the United Hebrew Benevolent Association (UHBA), the precursor to a full-fledged congregation and Temple. The president of the society, A. Wolf, stated in 1869 that the group had three aims: to have a consecrated burial ground and a funeral home; to aid its co-religionists who were in need, both in Helena and abroad; and to maintain worship services for the Jewish New Year and the Day of Atonement (the High Holy Days).

The cemetery was named "Home of Peace." A few of its stones still standing today indicate burials before official consecration of the land. By 1869 the United Hebrew Benevolent Association had also erected a funeral home. Wolf asserted more about the association in a speech:

> *The association has been in existence over two years and during that time has devoted thousands of dollars in relieving the distressed and afflicted. The association keeps constantly on hand several hundred dollars subject to the relief of all suffering persons worthy of the charity of the Order...You organized the Hebrew Benevolent Association in accordance with the strict enjoinment of the Holy Ordinances of Israel, named to relieve the distressed, support the afflicted, attend the sick and bury the dead, and you have aided your co-religionists beyond the broad seas—for as sure as you render assistance to your fellow men in the hour of distress so shall ye be blessed in this world and rewarded in the next to come by Him who is all goodness, all charity, and all merciful.*

The members of the society met regularly, and by 1872 the group had all the characteristics of a fraternal lodge. Its members met regularly at the Odd Fellows Hall, although an occasional extra meeting was held at a member's home or store. They started to record minutes on December 12, 1872, and the first order of business on that date was to admit Marcus Lissner to membership. The charter members were also listed in the notes: Edward Zimmerman, Sam Schwab, Herman Gans, Louis Kaufman, David Morris, Sam Levine, Adolph Birkenfeld, Jacob Loeb, Jack Herman, Ben Ezekiel, A. E. Davis, B. Alexander, Jacob Feldberg, Morris Silverman, Leopold Marks, Emil Lowenberg, Benjamin Pizer, Isaac Greenhood, Max Koleacker, Fernando Gans, Moses Morris, Isaac C. Marks, William J. Auerbach, Morris Sands, Julius Silverman, Wolf Sabolsky, Joseph Gans, Morris Goldberg, Abram Sands, Bernard Loeb, Henry Klein, Sol Poznanski, Max Sklower, and I. Bohm.

The next twenty years witnessed the growth of and the failure of a number of Jewish businesses in Helena, often because several family members joined together. Taking advantage of the large amount of money flowing from the gold fields, they established merchandising networks to the mines and surrounding communities. There were failures, too. As we look at the biographical sketches I have assembled, it will be apparent that some families came, moved, came back again, or left, completely broke. The overall economic climate affected Jewish-owned businesses as well as others, and the financial panic of the 1890s was particularly detrimental to Jewish-owned Helena banks.

Fire was another concern. Major fires swept the city, wiping out struggling businesses. Hotels were burned, mercantile stores lost all of their inventory, and some people had to start over again. Credit was often a problem. Helena Jews loaned money to businesses of all kinds, including some of the many houses of prostitution. Many of these loans were repaid, but some were not. Meanwhile, Jews often had difficulty obtaining credit for themselves; Jews were not considered a good credit risk by non-Jewish bankers, particularly in other parts of the country. Those lucky enough to have a network to draw on fared much better than those who did not.

The financially successful Jews invested in mining claims, cattle operations, and later in the beginnings of the oil business. By the late

Herman Gans family. Photo taken between 1890 and 1892, probably near Helena, Montana. Clockwise from Gans, standing in the center: Herman Gans, Lizzie Gans, Alice Gans, Morris Sands, Slurrocts or Slurrock (?), Harry ?, Bean ?, Sadie Gans, Rabbi Samuel Schulman, Rose Goldberg, Hattie Loble, Hattie Marks, Dave Marks, two unidentified women. COURTESY OF THE MONTANA HISTORICAL SOCIETY.

1880s there were fewer opportunities to start a new business in Helena, and many of the younger Jews became salesmen and clerks for those who had been there earlier. Indigent Jews who made their way to Helena were often given help by the United Hebrew Benevolent Association, then urged on their way. The arrival of the railroad in the 1880s helped expedite the movement of people and merchandise, and several important Helena Jewish families came at that time. Before the trains, merchandise was shipped up the Missouri River to Fort Benton, and then freighted overland by mule train, a grueling trip. Some of the early Helena Jewish residents made their living as freighters, a business full of economic risk. The first to get the cargoes when the ice broke up in the spring and the first to get the goods to Helena were able to charge the most. A slow freighter or one who ran into trouble might not be able to sell his goods for what he paid for them.

Jewish women in these early times were generally homemakers, responsible for raising children and keeping families strong. Tradition also gave them the responsibility for seeing that religion was observed in the home and that children learned the traditions of their heritage. Women were often responsible for taking care of the needy, so were an important arm of the United Hebrew Benevolent Association. On May 13, 1883, this was recognized as the Hebrew ladies of Helena were declared full members of the association.

With the women urging support, four years later, on May 8, 1887, the leaders of the Helena Jewish community decided that the time had come to solicit funds for a synagogue. The minutes of September 8, 1889, show that the UHBA was to "donate the *Sefer Torah* and the furniture, etc. belonging to them to the Congregation Emanu-El." On November 11, 1889, the *Helena Herald* reported that "the Israelites of this city have for the last two months been at work in organizing a congregation. They are now assured of success, and intend to send for a rabbi to officiate, and in less than three months expect to have weekly services. It is also their intention to build a synagogue at once which will be a credit to the Israelites as well as the city of Helena."

On October 2, 1890, the cornerstone of the building on North Ewing Street and Ninth Avenue was laid. Arrangements for the ceremony were made by Benjamin Harris and Edward Zimmerman. Governor Joseph K. Toole gave the principal address at the dedication of the building on Sunday, April 19, 1891, at four o'clock in the afternoon. The presentation of the Temple's key to the president of the congregation, Herman Gans, was made by Josephine Israel Hepner.

Helena's Temple was built of pink granite and dark pink mortar. It was two stories high and had large stained-glass windows all around. The basement was built so that it could be divided into several Sunday School and meeting rooms. The non-Jewish architects, Helein and Mathia of Helena, were responsible for the design, but the building committee consisted of Morris Silverman, Marcus Lissner, and Samuel Schwab. These three, plus Henry Klein and I. L. Israel were the first trustees of Congregation Emanu-El. The officers were Herman Gans, president; Jacob Feldberg, vice-president; Adolph Birkenfeld, secretary; and Jacob Loeb, treasurer.

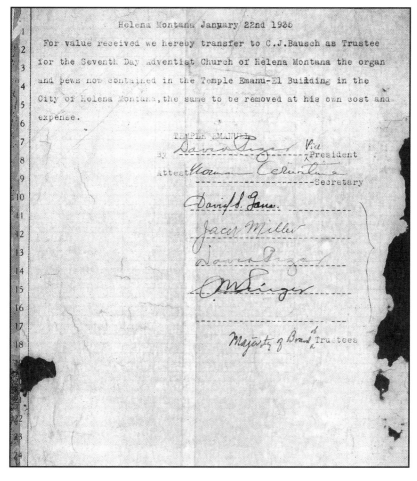

Deed of transfer of Temple Emanu-El organ and pews to the Seventh-Day Adventist church, Helena, January 22, 1935.

Congregation President Herman Gans was one of Helena's most successful businessmen. Soon after the congregation was established, Gans visited New York. While there he met Rabbi Samuel Schulmann and convinced him to accept a four-week trial period as Helena's rabbi. Schulmann, born in Russia, had emigrated to the United States as a boy, then studied in New York and in Berlin at Hochschule fur die Wissenschaft Judentems. He had absorbed the new ideas of German Reform Judaism and he brought those ideas with him to Helena.

Schulmann stayed in Helena for two years and was paid $2,300 a year. A fervent espouser of Reform Judaism, he wrote numerous letters on the subject. He influenced the Helena congregation to adopt German Reform ideas, and the congregation readily adopted the idea of no hats for the men during worship services and men and women sitting together. Since most of the Helena Jews were from a German background, their tendencies were already in that direction. Rabbi Schulmann accepted an offer to move to Kansas City in 1892, and eventually he became the rabbi at Temple Emanu-El in New York, the most prestigious Reform Temple in the United States. The Helena congregation sought another rabbi but was not able to attract one until 1901. Until then, lay members conducted services.

In retrospect, the building of the Temple came too late. Its completion came at a time when opportunities were dwindling for the merchants, and people were beginning to leave Helena. The acceptance of the Jews by the non-Jewish Helena community became another of the causes of the demise of the Jewish community since many intermarriages took place; religion was no longer the monolithic ideal it previously had been. New Jewish families were not attracted to the city after the Temple ceased its existence, and the desire to educate children out of state led to the eventual decline of the Helena Jewish community.

But for forty years the Jewish community of Helena flourished. In order to get a flavor of the Helena community and to see how its Jews fared, I have chosen to use personal interviews and research about selected Jewish families. The biographies presented here are merely a sampling, but they give the reader an idea of this unique early Montana Jewish community.

One of the earliest Montana Jewish settlers was Lewis Hershfield. Hershfield was American-born, at Utica in Oneida County, New York, on August 21, 1836. As an adult, he must have had some resources; he had the wherewithal to outfit and drive an ox team from Leavenworth, Kansas, to Colorado. Once there, he purchased twenty-six wagons full of dry goods and drove them from Central City, a Colorado mining town, through Denver and Salt Lake City, to Virginia City, Montana. He arrived there in July 1864.

Hershfield found a ready market for his goods, and he quickly sold them for gold dust. With his profits he established a bank, holding gold for miners afraid to send their treasure out for fear of the outlaw gangs attacking stagecoaches. He also served as a money exchanger, changing gold dust for cash.

When the exodus from Virginia City to the new boom town of Helena started, Hershfield moved his bank to Helena and became that city's leading banker. He was one of the many whose brother joined him in business; by 1882 the tax rolls of Lewis and Clark County (Helena) listed L. H. Hershfield and Brother as the fourth largest taxpaying concern. An ad in a Helena newspaper boasted of their wealth as well: "Values and Dimensions of the Mammoth Gold Bar the product of Vestel's Cast for the L. H. Hershfield and

Temple of Congregation Emanu-El, Helena. COURTESY OF THE MONTANA HISTORICAL SOCIETY.

Lewis H. Hershfield. PHOTO BY HOWARD J. LOWRY, COURTESY OF THE MONTANA HISTORICAL SOCIETY.

Bro. Bankers. Helena, Montana Ter., April 4, 1878. Length 20 inches. Depth $3^3/_4$ inches etc. Total 54,262.62."

An announcement in the same paper on May 10, 1882, said that the banking house of L. H. Hershfield and Brother would be succeeded on July 1 by the Mercantile National Bank of Helena with a capital stock of $250,000. The first board of trustees for the new Merchant's National Bank was composed of Lewis Hershfield and Aaron Hershfield, Thomas Cruse, Abram Sands, Absalom Davidson, Moses Morris, Silas S. Huntley, Charles Lehman, Nate Vestal, and W. D. Nichols, a mixture of Jews and non-Jews. The bank was the forerunner of the Union Bank of Helena.

The year 1889 marked the transition from territory to state for Montana. President Benjamin Harrison nominated the last territorial governor, and his choice was contrary to the advice of the Republican Party. According to newspaper reports, Benjamin F. White of Dillon was Harrison's nominee, but the party wanted Lewis Hershfield. White was apparently a compromise. The President's son, Russell Harrison, ran a newspaper in Helena, and he wanted Isaac D. McCutcheon of Helena to get the appointment. It was generally felt that he was trying to force Hershfield out of consideration for the post.

Hershfield lost another elective post when William Clark, a Democrat, was elected permanent chairman of the state constitutional convention by the thirty-nine Democrats while Hershfield received the thirty-five Republican votes.

The national banking crisis in the 1890s convinced Lewis's brother Aaron Hershfield to withdraw from Merchant's National Bank. He subsequently opened a new bank in Miles City, Montana, and fortunately was not affected when, on February 18, 1897, the Merchant's National Bank failed to open its doors, becoming the second Helena bank failure in four months. Governor Samuel Hauser's First National Bank had closed the previous September. By the next September, Hershfield's defunct bank declared a twenty-five percent dividend to all depositors, and in December it became the Union Bank and Trust Company, ending Hershfield's banking career.

Yetta and Bernice Lissner, whose father Marcus was an active member of both the Helena civic scene and Jewish community, were still living in Helena in 1966, when I interviewed them. Marcus Lissner was born in Prussia on January 17, 1834. He came to the United States in 1851, intending to head for Georgia, the home of an older brother of his who had emigrated earlier. The threat of the Civil War plus the lure of the West convinced him to set off for California instead, by way of the Isthmus of Panama. Lissner mined a little in California, then turned east to mine in Nevada and eventually move to Alder Gulch, Montana Territory, in July 1864, where he built a dredge and began to look for gold. He found enough to enable him to take his stake to the infant town of Helena where he went into the hotel business.

Lissner built the International Hotel on State and Main streets in Helena. It was one of the earliest hotels in the town, and was considered by some to be Helena's finest. The hotel expanded in a unique fashion. The original building was a three-story affair with a broad piazza and was near the theaters and the stagecoach office. An annex was built across the street and was connected by an enclosed second-story bridge. For a short time, Lissner owned the hotel in partnership with Max Sklower, but Sklower soon moved on to other hotel ventures. Fire was always a menace in early Helena, and the International Hotel and its annex were ablaze three times, in 1869, 1873, and 1874. The last blaze provided an excuse for Lissner to go east and order materials for the rebuilt buildings.

While on the trip, Lissner ordered fixtures and furnishings for the new home he was building. The residence he built at 315 East State was adorned with magnificent hand-carved panelling and sumptuous furniture. Although the International Hotel no longer exists, the home stands. I visited the home in 1966 when interviewing the two Lissner daughters, and its elegance was still apparent.

Marcus had come to Helena a single man, but when he had established his business he was ready for marriage and a family. He found his prospective bride in Helena, the daughter of Wolf Sabolsky. Sabolsky had come to Montana after Lissner, to become one of the territory's early freighters. After traveling up the Missouri River by boat, he continued the approximately one hundred and thirty miles between Fort Benton and Helena by wagon train, then stopped. On his trip to Montana, Sabolsky noticed that foodstuffs such as flour, salt, and other staples were highly priced and sold for gold dust or coin on delivery. If greenbacks were accepted at all, it was at fifty percent of face value. As an example of prices in the spring of 1865, flour for a short time was a dollar a pound. Before the coming of the railroad in 1883, the time of the year determined the price of merchandise: during winter months, the steamboats could not

Merchant's National Bank, Helena. COURTESY OF THE MONTANA HISTORICAL SOCIETY.

get to Fort Benton and supplies got short, so the prices zoomed up before the first boats arrived in the spring. The first new supplies to arrive brought the highest prices, prices that would then decline as freighters rushed their goods to the thawed-out mining camps. Sabolsky sold his goods in Helena, where he had built a cabin for his family. He had also fenced acreage in back of the cabin to hold and train wild horses, which he broke and sold to the army.

Sabolsky was one of the very few Jews in Helena who clung to his Orthodox beliefs. His wife would only eat Kosher food, and since it was not possible to obtain Kosher meat, she ate only vegetables. Together with the few other Orthodox Jews, they gathered at the Odd Fellows Hall to hold worship services and later used the schoolhouse on Warren Street. But in order to have his Orthodox daughter educated, Sabolsky sent her to St. Vincent's Academy, a Catholic school, since there were no public schools yet in Helena.

Sabolsky's daughter married Marcus Lissner in 1875 in a ceremony at his International Hotel. The Lissners had nine children, six girls and three boys. Bernice and Yetta Lissner recalled happy days as they were growing up. Since music was important to many of the Jewish families, and since Jewish children generally were expected to take music lessons, Marcus Lissner bought a piano. Shipping it from the East, upriver to Fort Benton, then freighting it to Helena was a costly venture, but it became the family treasure. The Lissner children and their friends gathered in the kitchen and, singing to the music of their new piano, learned to dance. Marcus Lissner was their teacher.

Yetta Lissner reminisced that music was important to many families. One night when one of her baby brothers became very ill, her mother and aunt ran across town to fetch Dr. Benjamin C. Brooke while Grandma Sabolsky watched the baby. The two young women were shivering and out of breath when they reached the doctor, and they had to sit and listen to the doctor's daughter Lalla play a piece on the piano before the doctor hitched up the sleigh and went back across town with the two women to treat the sick child.

Yetta and Bernice Lissner also recalled the other Jewish families they knew seemed to be especially conscientious about their children. They still remembered admonitions: "Jewish children don't behave like that," or "That's all right for someone else, but not for a Jewish child." Any family who could possibly afford it saw to it that their children had music and elocution lessons, and that they attended dancing school, which required white gloves and learning to walk through a receiving line. Yetta Lissner also recalled that the Jewish population supported theatrical productions and often sang and danced in them. They also helped bring in traveling troupes.

The Lissners prospered with their hotel and the Lissner Bottling Works. A spring discovered on some property they owned on West Main Street proved to contain a high mineral content, providing the impetus for the new business. Pipes were installed and a regular twice-weekly route was established to deliver Lissner Mineral Water.

Economic success and a sense of civic responsibility caused Marcus Lissner to run for alderman for Helena's first ward. He was constantly re-elected and remained in that position for eighteen years. James Lissner, who operated a liquor store in the International Hotel, succeeded his father on the council. James Lissner went on to serve one term in the state legislature as a Democratic representative from Lewis and Clark County.

Moses Morris and his brother David Morris were also among the Montana pioneers. They were born at Kempen, Duchy of Posen, Prussia, the sons of Joachim and Esther Schlesinger Morris. Moses Morris was born May 5, 1844; David Morris was born on November 8, 1849. The younger, David Morris, came to Montana first. He came to the United States in 1863, traveled to Denver, then made his way across the plains via the Lander Cut-off of the Oregon Trail and Soda Springs, Wyoming, to Virginia City, Montana. His brother Moses arrived alone in New York at age fourteen; when he was sixteen, he walked behind a wagon train from Leavenworth, Kansas, to Denver, Colorado. There he operated a small dry goods store and hoarded every penny he made. When he felt he had saved enough to travel to the new territory of Montana, he headed out. He unfortunately chose a light buggy as his vehicle and a rugged part of the winter to travel. Caught in a vicious snowstorm, he was lucky to be rescued before he froze to death. After his misadventure he finally joined his brother in Virginia City on May 1, 1864.

Within a short time, the Morris brothers moved to Helena. Their first business venture was making and selling crockery. Successful in the crockery business, they then established a mercantile business. Moses Morris used profits from the business to invest in real estate, banks, and cattle. In 1867, he built the first plastered residence in Helena.

The two brothers remained partners until 1888, when the business

Moses Morris. COURTESY OF THE MONTANA HISTORICAL SOCIETY.

was dissolved and David left Helena for a while. Moses retired from business forty years before his death and devoted himself to good works. He was initiated in the Masonic lodge just two years after he arrived in Montana in 1866, and when he died he was said to be the oldest living Mason in the state. He demitted from Lodge No. 3 in 1867 to become a charter member of King Solomon's Lodge No. 9, and he was Master of the Lodge for thirteen years, eight times in succession.

Moses Morris was also elected to the Helena City Council where he served for nine years, three of them as president of the council. He was treasurer of the Republican State Central Committee and corresponding treasurer of the Union League.

Religious affiliation was as important to Morris as civic responsibility, and he became the first president of the United Hebrew Benevolent Association. He served the Jewish community in whatever capacity he was needed. When the Temple was formed, he was also active with that group.

Another pioneer who went to Virginia City before settling in Helena was Benjamin Ezekiel. Ezekiel was born at Tiverton, Devonshire, England, in 1827, the son of Benjamin and Florence

Ezekiel. He arrived in the United States at age fourteen in 1841. Little is known about his wanderings in this country, but by 1863 he had drifted into Alder Gulch to mine for gold. He joined the Vigilante movement, which was devoted to ridding the area of the bandits who preyed on gold-laden stagecoaches and miners. Ezekiel was part of the group that helped to hang the infamous Sheriff Henry Plummer and his gang.

Ezekiel's political activities accompanied his other community interests. By 1865, Ezekiel had been elected commissioner of Madison County. Politics were rough-and-tumble, and during a heated political campaign, on February 26, 1874, *The Montanian* newspaper said:

> *Another editor attacked a candidate by saying, "The Charlatan and mounteback, Ben Ezekiel, writhing under the charges of fraud and guilt proved against him by this paper snaps and snarls like a belabored cur...prevents our taking further notice of the moral leper than to condescend to spit in his face should he cross our path."*

Ezekiel was elected to the legislature and served in the regular session, January 5, 1874. He also had served in the extraordinary eighth session, April 14, 1873 to May 8, 1873, and was chief clerk of the territorial House of Representatives for several terms. Since Ezekiel was deputy sheriff and a county commissioner, the newspaper attack seemed more an attack on political ideals than an anti-Semitic prejudice.

Two more men on the list of pioneers also wandered around like many others before arriving in Montana. Samuel Schwab, the son of Joseph M. and Metta Schwab, was born at Rimpar, Bavaria, Germany, on August 28, 1836. He came to the United States at age sixteen and rode the first stage between Salt Lake City, Utah, and Bannack, Montana Territory. Carrying with him goods to peddle to the miners, he arrived in Bannack on August 1, 1863.

Schwab's eventual son-in-law, Edward I. Zimmerman, the son of Aaron and Charlotte Zimmerman was born at Ortenberg, near Frankfort-on-the-Main, Germany, on March 20, 1838, just two years after his father-in-law. He came to the United States and wandered to California in 1855. From the California gold fields he made his way to William's Creek, California; Caribou, British Columbia (via Victoria, Vancouver Island); Portland, Oregon; Walla Walla, Washington; and then across the mountains via the Mullan Road to Blackfoot City, Montana, in 1864.

Both Schwab and Zimmerman eventually moved to Helena. Little is known about their families, but the two men owned and operated the Cosmopolitan Hotel in Helena and became charter members of the United Hebrew Benevolent Society. They worked hard to recruit other members.

The hotel was often the scene of civic affairs. In 1877, for instance, the owners hosted a party for the local soldiers who returned home after pursuing the fleeing Chief Joseph and the other Nez Perce Indians as they crossed Montana. In 1883, the hotel became the first four-story building in Helena when an extra floor was added.

Morris Silverman came from a border town between Russia and Poland in 1867. He made his way from New York to St. Louis, Missouri, then traveled overland by wagon with his two brothers. He left his wife and children in St. Louis until he could get settled, then arranged for them to follow him, by boat, to Fort Benton, Montana.

In Montana, the three Silverman brothers started a dairy farm but soon found that the farm could not support three families. They separated, and Morris Silverman moved to Helena. His daughter Dorothy Silverman reminisced many years later that her father not only sold supplies to the miners, but he always had a supply of candy on hand for the children who would come into his little store on Last Chance Gulch. Dorothy's memories of her father and early Helena focused on the newcomers to Helena who would invariably find her father's store and seek him out for some financial aid. She chuckled about one old reprobate know as "Jew Jake." He left a trunk in Morris's store to secure a loan he had made, but never returned for it. When they heard of Jake's death, the trunk was opened; the contents revealed a variety of gambling equipment and a wooden leg he had never worn.

Morris Silverman served as president of the United Hebrew Benevolent Association for many years. When he became too old to serve, he was elected honorary president because of his many years of faithful service. He was the main religious leader of the Helena Jewish community until they obtained the services of an ordained rabbi. He not only led services and taught Hebrew, but he circumsized male Jewish babies. His daughter was sure he had demonstrated his skill to a non-Jewish doctor, Dr. Brooke, who then began to perform the operation on some non-Jewish babies. Silverman also performed the ritual of Jewish weddings, although a civil ceremony had to be held to satisfy the requirements of the law. Lastly, he functioned as a *Shohet* (one who slaughters animals in a Kosher way) for the few Orthodox Jews who would only eat Kosher chicken. Dorothy also recalled that one of her father's best friends was the Reverend Father Lawrence Palladino, a Catholic religious leader. Palladino would come into the store, and the two would lean on the counter and talk for hours.

Dorothy Silverman was the youngest of the Silverman children, born in 1881, and was the only one of the family to be delivered by a doctor. The Silverman home was at 412 North Rodney, and was a three-story beauty, with the third floor often used by the children to perform Shakespearean plays. As with many of the Jewish families, books and theater were very important in their lives. Dorothy attended the University of Chicago School of Education and graduated in 1900. She returned to Helena after college and taught kindergarten. When that was discontinued by the Helena school district, she became a first-grade teacher, and continued in that capacity for thirty-seven years.

Dorothy Silverman's nephew, Joseph Sklower, son of Max and Betty Silverman Sklower, was born in Helena three weeks before his aunt on May 28, 1881. His mother was seventeen when he was born and was Dorothy's older sister. His father, Max, was a partner of Marcus Lissner in the ownership of the International Hotel. Joe Sklower lived in the hotel until he was four years old.

The Sklowers moved to White Sulphur Springs in 1886, and took over the ownership of the White Sulphur Springs Hotel. This hotel was the center of the big resort area in the 1880s, and in order to reach it, people boarded a stage in Helena at about four in the morning, rode all day, and arrived at the resort hotel about seven or eight o'clock in the evening. The stage would stop about every twenty miles to change horses, and the passengers would eat at the wayside stations which included Canyon Ferry and Diamond City, the latter being the halfway mark of the trip. Diamond City had started as a rich placer camp, but as the mines were tunneled beneath the town, the houses began to disappear on top, and the entire town was eventually abandoned.

The Sklowers remained in White Sulphur Springs for about fifteen years. When word of the Milk River project got around, the family decided there was an opportunity for a new hotel. They opened the Great Northern Hotel of Malta in 1904. They had to sell all they owned to establish the new venture, and the hotel kept Joe Sklower in Malta for the next forty-five years.

Joe Sklower had his high school education in Helena because there was no high school in White Sulphur Springs. He was interested in music and had become the owner of a cello in a roundabout way. His brother had brought it from eastern Montana where he had bought it from Charlie Kopps, a traveling music peddler. The brother tried to learn how to play, but could not master the instrument. Joe got it by default. About the same time that Joe became the owner of the cello, a group of wool buyers from Boston arrived at the White Sulphur Springs Hotel. They persuaded little Joe to try to play the cello so they could have their own little combo. He mastered the rudiments of playing, and then played by ear.

When Joe Sklower was sent to Helena for his education, he also became a music student of Madam Ericka, a Bohemian who provided music for most of the city's social events. She appeared at weddings, theatrical productions, and receptions. She and her little orchestra would sit behind large ferns and provide "genteel" music. She also taught music.

Three Jewish graduates were among the Helena High graduating class of 1899—Marvin Gans, Lillian Lissner, and Joseph Sklower. An excerpt from the book *From the Quarries of Last Chance Gulch* gives a glimpse of the social activities enjoyed by the more affluent Helena families, both Jewish and non-Jewish:

> *The judicious use of Turkish rugs, settees, piano lamps, and sofa pillows added immeasurably to the appearance of the large hall. The juniors, and hosts and hostesses of the evening received their guests in an artistic little reception room, the entrance to which was through an archway of evergreen. On passing into the hall each guest was handed a dainty program in the class colors, blue and gold.*

At the described dance given by the junior class to honor the senior class, music was provided by Madam Ericka's orchestra, and frappé was served from large cut-glass punch bowls. The class of twenty-seven was the largest in the history of Helena High.

Joe Sklower attended the Colorado School of Mines after graduation, and then went on to the University of California where he received his degree. He returned to Montana and joined his family, who had recently moved to Malta.

Liege Smith, a Malta banker, proposed the formation of a town band during the winter of 1904, and all citizens were invited to join. The prospective band members each chose an instrument from a pile, and newcomer Sklower got what was left, a clarinet. He learned to play it by ear, practicing in the bank vault because the hotel guests objected to his initial efforts at his home in the hotel. Since the bank president was an ardent member of the band, and the group needed a clarinet player, the vault seemed to be an ideal solution to the problem of practice space. The band gained local fame by playing at concerts and dances. They almost precipitated an international incident when they were invited to play at Val Marie, Canada, and they played "The Star Spangled Banner" instead of "God Save the King" as an encore.

When the Homestead Act was passed, one of the real estate men happened to ask Sklower if he had ever used his homestead rights. Sklower replied, "No," then pondered the matter. He decided he might as well file on some land, so in 1907 he filed on 160 acres two miles from Malta and worked to prove it up. When he finally left Malta in 1948 to become secretary of the Chamber of Commerce of Glasgow, he got more money for the farm than he did for the hotel.

Many early Montana biographical compilations have a biography of H. Sol Hepner. Hepner was the first boy to graduate from Helena High, in 1885, just three years after he arrived in Helena from Russia. Sol Hepner was born in Tzaritzin, Russia, on February 25, 1869. His father Barnett Hepner came to the United States in 1871, but the family remained in Europe until they were sent for. Work in Pennsylvania and Colorado enabled Barnett to save enough money to open a store in Helena and send for his wife Bertha and his children, Sol, Jennie, and Luba, in 1882.

Sol Hepner's early education was at the Imperial Pro-Gymnasium in Russia. After graduating from Helena High, he worked for Colonel Broadwater's Montana National Bank for four years to earn enough money to enable him to attend the University of Michigan Law School. He graduated from there in 1891 then returned to Helena, where he worked in several law offices. He later opened his own practice with offices in the Union Bank building.

Hepner served as a representative to the state legislature from 1897 to 1899, was the county prosecuting attorney from 1909 to 1910, and was Helena city attorney from 1911 to 1912. He was an active Democrat and a dedicated Mason, serving as Grand Master of the Grand Lodge of Masons in Montana from 1903 to 1904. He also served as patron of the Order of Eastern Star and as president of the Algeria Temple of the Mystic Shrine, and led the Helena Lodge No. 193 of Elks and the Independent Order of Odd Fellows. Giving up a year of law practice, he served as President Woodrow Wilson's appointee to the District Exception Board No. 1 for Montana, serving as chairman until he was honorably discharged in 1919.

In 1899, Sol Hepner married Josephine Israel, whose family had come to Helena from San Francisco in 1879. The wedding was reported on the society page of the Helena newspaper; the ceremony was held at the Israel home, 22$^1/_2$ North Park Avenue, with District Judge Henry C. Smith officiating. The couple went east for their honeymoon, combining the event with the annual session of the Imperial Council of the Shrine which was being held in New York City.

Josephine Israel Hepner taught elocution at Montana Wesleyan University in the Helena valley before her marriage. She became a worthy grand matron of the Grand Chapter, Order of the Eastern Star of Montana, and the new Helena chapter was named after her on March 20, 1920. She founded and served as president of the Montana Children's Home, and was the first woman to be appointed to Helena's Public Library Board. She was also vice-president of the Montana Historical Society from 1922 to 1923.

The couple had two children, Claire Algeria Hepner, born in 1900, and Harold Steffan Hepner, born in 1904. In addition to their heavy involvement in political and civic affairs, they were also active in the United Hebrew Benevolent Association. They exemplified the integration of many Jewish families into the religious and cultural affairs of the capital city.

"We weren't pioneers. My father came to Helena on the first train in 1883," said Frieda Fligelman. Her father, Herman Fligelman, was born in Romania; when he arrived in Boston accompanied by a friend, the two of them had twenty dollars between them. They found work in restaurants and on the docks, and they worked their way westward by laying streetcar tracks. Herman saved enough to buy some goods to peddle, and he learned English as he sold and worked his way toward Helena.

In Montana, the peddling led to the establishment of a store with three partners: Robert Heller, Henry Loble, and George Frankfort. Heller and Loble roomed at Wolf Sabolsky's, Yetta Lissner's grandfather, an example of how the Jewish community developed ties to one another. The new store was called the New York Store; it later became Fligelman's. It was located on the main floor of the International Annex in the 1880s.

When fire hit the building in 1887, the New York Store lost $25,000 worth of merchandise. It was only insured for $5,000, so the young partners faced quite a setback.

Lewis Hershfield saw some possibilities for the store, and he staked Herman Fligelman to a trip East to buy the latest goods. Herman's return trip to Helena was a memorable one because the train was held up about sixty miles east of Billings by a dozen armed and masked robbers, and the train was delayed for about an hour and a half while the passengers were searched for valuables. Hershfield's investment proved to be a wise one, for the store prospered and Fligelman's grew to be Helena's leading department store until it was sold in 1959.

Fligelman had two daughters, Frieda and Belle. His wife died in childbirth when Belle was born, and some aunts were brought from Romania to raise the girls. Within a few years, Fligelman remarried. His second wife was Getty Vogelbaum of Germany. Frieda remembered that her father was always collecting money for something, especially for victims of pogroms in Russia. He and his brothers would play pinochle and put the winnings in a box to save for a big family picnic, but they would hear of a pogrom, and the money would be sent to help the unfortunate Europeans.

Getty Fligelman worked with the other ladies of the Jewish community in the United Hebrew Benevolent Association, and when poor itinerant Jews arrived in Helena, she would often borrow a horse and buggy, make the rounds of the Jewish families for donations of food, clothing and a little money, give it to the family, and urge them on their way. "No one was ridiculously rich, but no one was poor among us," said Frieda.

Belle Fligelman wrote of an episode in the lives of her sister and herself involving Tommy Cruse, a rugged and unschooled miner who became a millionaire and a well-known banker in Helena. She told that Warren Dahler, son of a pioneer banker and miner, and his younger brother Gerald, converted the woodshed in their backyard into a small theater, complete with stage and a curtain that could be raised and lowered. He gathered a cast of neighborhood children ages eight to fourteen, and, with himself as star, produced a pruned version of *Hamlet*. Mamie Cruse, Cruse's thirteen-year-old, only daughter played Ophelia, and the two Fligelman girls played ladies in waiting, dressed in some of Mamie's finery.

The opening (and closing) night saw a packed house including U.S. Senator Thomas H. Carter and his family (his sons were cousins of Mamie Cruse). Cruse was so pleased that he announced he was taking the show on the road. The following week, the cast and their mothers were taken to Marysville to Cruse's famous Bald Mountain Mine to put on the show for the miners.

As recounted in the *Great Falls Tribune* of November 24, 1963, Belle Fligelman recalled:

> *Our mothers packed our satchels and we started trouping. Colonel Cruse chartered the train that went from Helena to Marysville three days a week, and we all piled in. The trip was several hours over what seemed a perilous road. The tracks wound around a steep mountainside on a wooden trestle, and the squeaking was frightening. The mother of Queen Gertrude was on her knees in the aisle praying earnestly that the trestle would hold. Her prayers were answered.*

The miners cheered the show, and the cast and their mothers stayed in the Drumlummon Hotel for two weeks as guests of Colonel Cruse.

Frieda Fligelman never married. Her sister Belle graduated from the University of Wisconsin with a B.A. in 1913 and worked for a year as editor of the *Montana Progressive*. She and her sister were strong advocates of women's suffrage; years later, Frieda recalled marching down Fifth Avenue in New York City during a women's suffrage parade and seeing the arrests made during the demonstration. She strongly supported women's rights all her life. Belle Fligelman was publicity manager for Jeanette Rankin's successful campaign for the United States House of Representatives.

Belle was married in New York on April 30, 1918, to Norman Winestine, an educated man who was born in Wassaic, Duchess County, New York, on February 15, 1895. Winestine was schooled at Waterbury, Connecticut, Yale University (B.A. 1914), Columbia University in New York, the University of Pennsylvania, and Dropsie College in Pennsylvania. The Winestines settled in Helena after their marriage, and in 1931, Norman became president of Fligelman's department store. The store had been destroyed by a spectacular fire in 1928, and Winestine not only rebuilt the store but was instrumental in changing the name of Helena's Main Street to Last Chance Gulch, marking the historical interest of the area. During the years of the Great Depression, he served as secretary of the Montana State Recovery Board under the National Recovery Administration, having been appointed by President Franklin D. Roosevelt. He was also president of the Helena Chamber of Commerce and was active in many local civic organizations. A member of the Helena school board for five years, he was a Mason and president of the Montana Historical Society.

Louis Kaufman was born in Baden, Germany, but left home at the age of sixteen and arrived in New York. An adventurous young man, Kaufman was fascinated with the idea of mining for gold, and he inquired about the western gold camps, learning that travel to the newly named Montana Territory was extremely difficult. The region had been part of the Louisiana Purchase, and the best information about the area came from the journals of the Lewis and Clark expedition, which had crossed the territory more than fifty years previously. To get to Montana, one could travel west by train, switch to stagecoach for sixteen days, then face three to six months of travel by mule and oxen teams. The capitals of the neighboring territories to the east, Yankton in Dakota Territory, and Omaha, in the state of Nebraska, were both on the Missouri River, and were both sixteen to twenty days distant by steamboat, the fastest means of travel. West, in Idaho Territory, the capital was at Lewiston, still a week away from the early Montana settlements.

Kaufman decided it would be easier to get to California first. From California, he made his way east to Montana and soon began mining in the Alder Gulch area. Within six years, he had switched from mines to merchandise, investing his profits in the Helena Meat Company, with Louis Stadler as his partner. Both young men began investing in the cattle business, and soon they were owners of the Kaufman and Stadler Ranch.

Bad weather plagued the partners, and in November 1881, they lost a valuable herd of cattle when they were being driven across the frozen Missouri River at a crossing place called Canyon Ferry. The ice gave way under the load of animals; thirty-four were drowned. Kaufman and his two helpers barely saved themselves. Five years later, the ranchers struggled through the famed winter of 1886, long remembered as Montana's worst. Kaufman visited his ranch in the Judith Basin during the middle of that terrible winter and noticed a Texas brindle cow that seemed to be hanging around. He commented about the animal to Jesse Phelps, his foreman, before he went back to Helena. Phelps had company that winter—a young cowboy named Charley Russell, who spent the cold months tending cattle with Phelps. During the severest part of the winter, when Kaufman's cattle were dying in wholesale numbers, the cowboys tending them were getting despondent over the huge losses sustained by the herds. Kaufman wrote

Louis E. Kaufman. COURTESY
OF THE MONTANA HISTORICAL
SOCIETY.

from Helena asking about conditions at the ranch, and Phelps did not
have the heart to tell Kaufman the whole truth. While he pondered over
his report, Russell got an idea. He took out the watercolors he packed
around with him, and on a small piece of paper (about two by four inches),
he sketched a starved-looking cow, showing the Kaufman-Stadler Bar R
brand, standing humped over the snow—the Texas brindle cow that
Kaufman had commented on earlier in the season. Hungry coyotes waited
impatiently for the steer to drop. Russell signed his sketch, "Waiting for a
Chinook." Russell mailed the painting to Kaufman without any further
explanation.

The watercolor caused much excitement in Helena, and Kaufman
subtitled it *Last of the Five Thousand.* It brought fame to Russell and was
widely copied. A later version of the picture hangs in the Russell Gallery
of the Montana Historical Society in Helena.

The Hirshberg family joined the
Helena congregation, but its members settled in several areas of Montana.
Joseph Hirshberg, the family patriarch, was born in Posen, Germany, on
January 28, 1847. He came to the United States in 1863 and made his

way from New York to California, travelling through the Isthmus of Panama to get to the West Coast. Once there, he worked for a short time as clerk in a dry goods store, then bought a small load of goods and traveled about peddling. In 1864, he and a friend took a team and a load of dry goods to Salt Lake City, selling along the way. With the money they earned, Joe opened a small store in Smithfield, in the Cache Valley of Utah. Within a year, he was eager to move on again, so he sold the Utah store and opened another in Lincoln Gulch, Montana, with Louis Caro as a partner. By 1874, when Hirshberg moved to Helena, he had also started and sold a store in Cedar Creek, Montana.

From 1875 to 1878, Hirshberg engaged in both the cattle and mercantile business in the Flathead Lake region. He even took a load of cattle to Canada to sell to the Indians there. He returned to Helena, but wanderlust again set in and he headed for New York. There he met Eva Davis, who was also born in Posen, Germany, but ten years later, on April 1, 1857. The two were married on January 5, 1878.

After his marriage, Hirshberg began a new phase of his business career. Forming a partnership with Arge Nathan, he bought a large supply of goods in the east and shipped it by rail to Bismarck, North Dakota, then by steamer up the Missouri River to Fort Benton, Montana. The newly married couple arrived in Fort Benton in May 1879 and opened a store on Front Street to sell their transported goods. The partnership between Hirshberg and Nathan lasted until 1887, when Hirshberg bought Burd and Armstrong, a general store in Choteau. In 1889, Hirshberg closed the Fort Benton store and divided his interests between Choteau and the sheep business, with the help of his brother Julius Hirshberg who came to manage the store in Choteau that same year.

By 1894, Joe Hirshberg had opened another store in Dupuyer, in Teton County, Montana, putting his cousin Carl Harris in charge. Hirshberg retained interests in the stores but spent his time raising sheep on the Belknap Indian Reservation in the Bears Paw Mountains. He ran a large number of Rambouillet sheep on government land, and did well in the wool business.

Joe and Eva Hirshberg had four sons, all born in Fort Benton: Edward, born in 1880; Sidney, born in 1881; Mortimer, born in 1883; and Frank, born in 1889. As parents, Joe and Eva felt they had to move to Helena so the boys could be educated. They succeeded. In 1901 *Progressive Men of the State of Montana* said of Hirshberg, "He had an excellent wife and cultivated sons." The article about the Hirshbergs also mentioned that the family was active in the social and civic affairs of Helena.

Sands Brothers Dry Goods store, 1907. COURTESY OF THE MONTANA HISTORICAL SOCIETY.

The vast opportunities offered in the West figure in the rise and decline of another family's fortunes. Samuel Cohen was born in New York City in 1837. As a young man, he was apprenticed to learn the jewelry and brush maker trades, and he worked at these for seven years. Seeking new opportunities, he made his way to Bannack, Montana, where he established the first clothing and men's furnishings house in the boomtown. Soon he opened a branch in the newer mining community of Virginia City.

In 1872, Cohen returned to New York, where he married seventeen-year-old Yetta Posnanski. The couple lived in New York for several years as Cohen looked after his investments, but a financial panic on the stock market caused him to lose most of his money, and he again looked to the West to make another fortune. The newest mining area was at Leadville, Colorado, so Cohen headed in that direction. Again a mercantile establishment got him started, and this time he invested his profits in real estate. Depression hit once more, though, and again he was wiped out. Since a move seemed to be imperative, the Cohens returned to New York. But within a short time western fever hit Sam again, and this time the family moved to Helena. Cohen again opened a store, and this one suceeded: he remained in business in Montana for twenty years. Sam Cohen was one of the small group of Orthodox Jews in Helena.

Lew Allen Cohen, his eldest son, was born in New York and educated both there and in Helena. When he was sixteen, he decided to become self-supporting so went to work for Sands Brothers as a bookkeeper. In 1893, he became department manager for Sands, what was then the oldest established dry goods house in Montana. By 1907, the company was reorganized and Cohen was named president. He married Yetta Feldberg, daughter of Helena pioneer Jacob Feldberg.

Gans and Klein store on the northeast corner of Broadway and Main, Helena, Montana. COURTESY OF THE MONTANA HISTORICAL SOCIETY.

Jewish pioneer Joseph Gans operated another Helena department store. The following ad for the Gans and Klein store appeared in the *Helena Independent* on October 3, 1897:

FALL STYLES IN BOYS CLOTHING
Fancy Tartan vestee suit, braided collar, a handsome suit.......$8.00
Fancy Zouava coat, an improvement on the "reefer"........$11.00
Blue Serge suit, embroidered vest.....$7.00
Fancy Covert Cloth box coat: very warm and stylish....$7.50
The "Gunboat Helena" suit, navy serge, pennants embroidered on vestee— a home novelty.....$8.75
All wool chenille Reefer, wool-lined, a very warm garment...$4.00
SUITS FROM $1.00   REEFERS FROM $2.00

Gans and Klein ads appeared widely in Montana papers and magazines. The president of the firm, Joseph Gans came to Montana in 1866 and experienced the life of freighter, rancher, stockman, and merchant.

The youngest of fifteen children, Gans was born in Neustadt, German Bavaria (Austria), and came to New York in January 1861. Within a year he had crossed the Panamanian Isthmus and made his way to California, where he stayed for six months. Oregon and a job in a butcher shop came next, then a two-year stint in Boise, Idaho, where he helped operate a pack train. After a short trip to Canada, he found himself in Helena in December 1866. There he started with a store at the Jefferson Bridge, then branched out from merchandising to cattle ranching. His range was the Bears Paw Mountains; his brand was the XIT.

Gans formed a partnership with Klein in 1876. By 1882, the partners were the sixth-largest taxpayers in Lewis and Clark County. Gans then turned his attention to sheep-raising in Wyoming; he was soon one of that state's leading sheep men. He was active in the Helena Jewish community, and was a master of King Solomon Masonic Lodge No. 9 and its treasurer for thirty-five successive terms.

Governor Benajmin F. Potts officiated at the marriage of Joseph Gans and Frederika Kaufman on November 26, 1876, an event well-marked in the local press.

A well-known professional man in Helena was Dr. Louis Fligman, a cousin of the Fligelmans. (Somewhere in the passage from Romania to New York the spelling of the name changed.)

The son of a small clothing store owner in Butte and Helena, he epitomized the second generation of Jewish immigrants.

Fligman was born in Berlad, Romania, on May 20, 1878. He came to the United States as a child and was educated in Minnesota. On graduating from high school in 1894, he entered the University of Minnesota. After completing his undergraduate work there, he instructed physiological chemistry while he attended medical school. He established his medical practice in Helena in 1903, then went to Europe a year later for postgraduate work in internal medicine and nervous diseases at the University of Vienna. The next few years found him alternating medical practice in Helena and attending European schools for more intensive training. He studied at the universities of Paris, London, Padua (Italy), and Berne (Switzerland) and became proficient in the languages of the countries he studied in.

From 1905 to 1907, Dr. Fligman was president of the Helena Board of Health.

Lester Henry Loble was a Helena attorney, businessman, and judge of the first Montana Judicial District. Loble was born in 1892 to Henry and Hattie Marks Loble.

Lester's father, Henry Loble, was one of the original parners in the New York Store, a Helena department store, and was president of that enterpise until his death in 1913. He was active in Temple Emanu-El, a member of the Montana Club, and an active Mason. Lester's mother, Hattie, was a Montana native, born in Diamond City in 1871, the daughter of Leopold and Clara Marks. Leopold Marks fought for the Confederacy in the Civil War; his brother fought for the Union. Leopold lost everything he had during the war, so he struck out acorss the country with a covered wagon, ending his journey at Fort Benton. He arrived there on July 4, 1867, with his wife, daughter, and three sons. They all moved to Diamond City a short time later, and still later to White Sulphur Springs, where Marks established a mercantile business, became active in the community, and became a county commisioner.

Henry Loble and Hattie Marks were married at Temple Emanu-El in Helena on November 18, 1891. Their son Lester attended Helena schools, Cascadilla School in Ithaca, New York (graduating in 1911), and New York University Law School. He was admitted to the Montana Bar on December 24, 1914. His son, a graduate of Stanford University and the Montana School of Law, became his partner.

Before becoming a judge, Lester Loble was an alderman, state legislator, city and county attorney, and state chairman of the Democratic Party. He was also a Mason, Odd Fellow, and president of the Helena Chamber of Commerce.

One Jew who had an impact on early Helena but was only there for a short time was Joseph Soss, who designed the state capitol. An architect and builder, Soss was awarded the contract to build the impressive public building. He arrived in Helena in 1898. He and his family spent six years in the city as he built a replica of the national Capitol. The Helena building was of gray sandstone from the Columbus quarries of Yellowstone County, Montana. The quarries were operated by the Montana Sandstone Company, incorporated by Joseph Soss, H. Sol Hepner, and B. Hagar.

Soss was alert to other business opportunities in Montana, and although the first commercial oil discoveries in the state were made in 1916, the July 1901 issue of *The Rocky Mountain Magazine* had the following article:

> *Joseph Soss of Helena, and E. R. Poindexter of Dillon, returned Monday from a trip to the oil fields of Kintla Lake and McDonald's Lake, says the* Kalispell Bee. *They are interested extensively in the new fields, Mr. Soss being an expert upon whose report a great deal depends. He claims to have visited every oil region of any consequence in the world, from Roumania to Ohio, and was the original discoverer of the Ohio oil region. California and Texas discoveries being recent, Mr. Soss has not visited them, but he is enthusiastic over the outlook for oil in quantities in this region. In his opinion, the oil field extended from Kintla and McDonald Lakes up to our very doors and when development is once taken up and pushed, the Flathead Valley will be the most productive oil region in the United States. His trip to the lakes was a hard one, through fallen timber and almost inaccessible trails, the continuous rain not helping any, but he is glad he went, because he is well satisfied with the prospects for oil.*
>
> *The Butte Company is building a road in from Kintla Lake to McDonald and when it is finished, machinery for boring wells will be taken in by several companies. The best locations, Mr. Soss thinks, are within ten miles of the lakes, but oil is everywhere. The wells are probably going to have to be drilled from eight to twelve hundred feet, but he*

Montana State Capitol at Helena, as it looked when it was completed by Joseph Soss, in 1902. COURTESY OF THE MONTANA HISTORICAL SOCIETY.

thinks the oil will flow from here in quantities which will make the region famous.

About ten square miles of placer ground has been taken up by his company which has the men in the field more than doubling the amount of the location. The country in that immediate vicinity is about all taken up now, and there is little else to do but wait for the completion of the wagon road so that machinery can be taken in.

In common with other experts who have been about here investigating, Mr. Soss cannot realize why Kalispell people have not gone into this good thing. The oil comes to the surface in the width off the lakes but there is a strong possibility that the reserves extend all over the basin and a greater depth than about the lakes. Under the present conditions, it is not likely that more development work will be done this year, but after the machinery once gets in and oil is found in paying quantities the capital will be forthcoming.

Actually, oil seepages were found around Kintla Lake in 1892, in the extreme northern end of what was then Missoula County, four miles south of the Canadian border, and when Soss got interested in 1901, the area again caused some excitement. Several Butte men formed the Butte Company, a Helena group formed the Kintla Oil Company, and a Kalispell group financed the Kintla Lake Oil Company, but the excitement died down again when they were unable to get commercial production.

Soss moved on to Butte after he finished the state capitol, where he contracted more building projects. He also invented a concealed hinge, patented it, and formed a Butte company to manufacture it. The project proved very successful, and Soss moved to New York, and then finally to Detroit, where his hinges were widely used on automobile doors.

There were many other Jews in Helena. These few representatives show the backgrounds, family patterns, and accomplishments of some of those who helped build the city and the congregation and who, along with unnamed others, were responsible for the first organized Jewish community in Montana.

CHAPTER TWO

BUTTE

Butte and Helena both began as typical western mining towns in the 1860s and 1870s. Placer mining in both places attracted individual miners who were usually young and adventuresome and who were looking for a stake to help build their fortunes. Helena grew from this beginning to become a thriving city and state capital. Butte grew, too, but its growth was forced in another direction.

From 1864 to 1865, there were about 150 men working placer discoveries along Silver Bow Creek, a small mountain stream near the area that would become Butte. The creek's shallow deposits were worked out quickly and the mining camp faced extinction as discouraged miners moved away. The remaining men knew they needed a grand scheme to attract men and capital or face their camp becoming a ghost town. Quartz gold and silver became the focus of their campaign, and a hard-hitting public relations drive was launched to attract men and money to Butte. The determined Butte boosters were successful, and by 1875 the town was a busy, prosperous place.

Copper soon displaced silver and gold in importance, and Butte became known as "The Richest Hill on Earth." With Butte's emphasis on hard-rock mining and copper ore, which required vast quantities of dirt to produce even a ton of copper, it was clear that a different type of miner was needed. People flocked to the mountain area from all over the world, but those who wanted to go into business seldom used the mines as a way to accumulate capital. Instead, they worked for others who had money, such as the famed industrial "copper kings" William Clark, Augustus Heinze, and Marcus Daly, or started small businesses to serve the hard-rock miners.

As Butte boomed between 1888 and 1900, many people who had not become financially successful in Helena moved to the huge, new city to try a new approach. In 1880, Butte had 3,364 people and Helena had 3,630. Helena had its largest growth in the 1890s, swelling to 14,000 people, but by 1900, Butte had grown to 30,470—with some estimates ranging much higher—and Helena numbered only 10,770. Montana's merchants moved to where the people were.

The Butte Jewish community was a blend of immigrants from both eastern and western Europe. German Jews arrived there first, and they were the ones who ultimately formed the Reform congregation. These first Jews to arrive in Butte, mostly Germans, were dubbed "the four hundred."

The next tide of Jewish immigration resulted from pogroms in eastern Europe, and it brought Jews from Russia, Romania, Hungary, and Galicia, a region covering parts of southern Poland and the Ukraine. These later settlers arrived in the largest cities of the eastern U. S., then trickled westward. They brought with them the social chasm that existed in Europe between German Jews and Jews of eastern Europe. Many of the newcomers were devoutly Orthodox in their religious practices at a time when the Reform movement was growing in Butte. The social cleavage that resulted lasted well into the twentieth century. In the 1960s, when I spoke to representatives of both groups of Jews, the Orthodox referred to the Reform group as "them" or "they," rather than using names. Comments such as: "Oh, he's a member of the other group; he only knows one side of what happened in Butte," or, "Be sure to talk to one of our people. 'They' don't

Butte, Montana. Courtesy of the Montana Historical Society.

41

know what went on." Or, "How could [Rabbi] Kelson write about the Jews of Butte [in his master's thesis], when he never talked to any of us?"

From its beginnings, Butte was a raucous mining town, open day and night. Miners made and spent money as fast as they could, and budding politicians soon aligned in groups that eventually would be powerhouses in state government. The town was wild, as Jewish novelist Myron Brinig noted in the title of one of his books on Butte, *Wide Open Town*. Rows of cribs lined the streets and alleys in the center of town as prostitutes plied their trade. Some women who lived in Butte in the "old days" said that because of "the girls," Butte was the safest place in the world for a "real lady." Sin was so easily accessible that "nice" women did not have to worry about being molested, they argued.

Jewish landlords owned some of the property that housed the cribs and Jewish girls worked one part of the street. Many of these girls were recent European immigrants who found prostitution a good way of making a living in the untamed town. Some finished their lives in the trade, but others married and eventually became respected members of the community. The Jewish girls were noted for a special habit: they closed up shop for the Jewish High Holy Days. "Never on Sunday" became "Never on Rosh Hashanah or Yom Kippur" in Butte.

Jewish heritage sometimes came to the fore in unexpected ways. Jew Kate, one of "the girls," married her pimp, a gambler named Curly Darrow who was a non-Jew and the son of an Episcopal minister. When Curly died, he requested burial next to Kate, who had preceded him in death. The funeral was conducted by a minister, but Darrow was placed at rest in the Jewish cemetery. Leo Kenoffel, one of the pallbearers, intoned traditional Hebrew prayers. Another "girl" known as Black-haired Rosie asked for Jewish pallbearers in her will; at her funeral the only Jews present were the pallbearers and the Jewish layman who read the services. She did not join the Jewish community during her life, but joined it at her death.

Nicknames were widely used among the prostitutes, and they often revealed interesting tidbits about the person they identified. Jean Davis tells this story in *Shallow Diggin's*:

> Among those bearing colorful nicknames were two ladies of the shadows who were reputed to be the world's slickest "dips." The first of these, Jew Jess, lived in Butte for many years. An old newspaper account tells of her prowess.

Frank Hickman had a sandwich shop. A sheepherder stopped and bought a sandwich. He started east on Galena Street and a few yards from Hickman's place he was stopped by a frail dark woman, holding a cigarette in one hand, who asked him for a match.

As the sheepherder handed her the match, she lifted a pocketbook from the inside of his coat. With a movement so adept and yet so swift as to defy observation, the woman who was Jew Jess, slipped the wallet to a Negro woman. The latter, however, was a bungler, and the sheepherder got the flash of his wallet.

He pulled a revolver and shot near the Negro woman's feet. With a scream of terror, she dropped the wallet and ran. The stranger picked up his pocketbook, and stepping to Hickman's door, counted the contents. It contained $999. "It's all here," he said. "I came to town with a thousand dollars, and I spent one dollar." Meanwhile Jew Jess had disappeared as completely as though the sidewalk had swallowed her.

"I wonder how in hell that nigger got my wallet," the rube said to Hickman. "She must have got it when I gave the little woman a match."

One of the scandals of early Butte involved two Jewish men who never joined any of the Jewish congregations, but who were publicly known as Jews. Harry Deutch and Max Freud became defendants in a white slavery case. Freud owned property on the prositute's row, called "the line," and the two men had been bringing girls to Butte to work in the cribs. Although Butte Jews protested that the men did not really belong to the Butte Jewish community, the men belonged to the B'nai B'rith lodge. Lodge members were so aghast at the white slavery charges that they instituted proceedings to expel the two men from B'nai B'rith for moral reasons. A full-fledged trial took place in San Francisco. William Meyer, a Jewish Butte attorney, filed the briefs. A heated trial ensued, and the men were found guilty and expelled from B'nai B'rith for moral reasons, an act unprecedented in the history of the District Four lodge.

Max Freud was one of Augustus Heinze's lieutenants, and he helped to manage the ABC Hotel where many of the prostitutes lived. He also ran some flophouses, charging fifteen cents a bed, with a rapid turnover in the use of the beds. Heinze, who figures prominently in Butte's political and economic "war of the copper kings" also employed another Jew, Abe Cohen, who was in charge of getting votes in some of Butte's turbulent elections. For five dollars a vote, Cohen was able to keep a steady stream of men coming from the flophouses to the polls. Aided by names gathered from the cemetery, he guaranteed three to four votes per flophouse resident.

Butte was a mixture of many religions, and in a single block a synagogue and several churches could coexist. Those who were children in the town's early days recalled that they might go to synagogue on Saturday and invite non-Jew friends, then in turn go to church on Sunday with their friends. This peaceful coexistence can be seen throughout the years. For instance, when the Reform congregation first gathered in Butte, it held services in the First Presbyterian Church on the southwest corner of Idaho and Galena streets. Later, in 1925, when the Jewish congregation had its own building, the Presbyterians were burned out of their sanctuary. Minister Eiko J. Groenvald and his congregation were invited to hold their services in the Temple until their church could be repaired.

A Hebrew Benevolent Association of Butte preceded the formal organization of a congregation, much as it had in Helena. In 1881, the association held Butte's first High Holy Day services. When congregations were formed, though, one was not enough. The diverse backgrounds of Butte's Jews required two congregations, one Reform and one Orthodox. Before long the Orthodox congregation split in two again, so Butte had three Jewish congregations.

The railroad donated land to the three major religious groups in Butte—Catholics, Protestants, and Jews—and three cemeteries resulted: St. Patrick, Mount Moriah, and B'nai Israel. According to court records, the Northern Pacific Railroad deeded land for B'nai Israel to the Hebrew Benevolent Association in 1885. Trustees accepting the tract were Joseph Rosenthal, David S. Cohen, and Jack Kahnweiler. By 1893, title was in the hands of Henry Jonas, and the Columbia placer claim was located within the boundaries of the cemetery. Jonas was an active member of the congregation and apparently turned the deed over to the congregation once it had incorporated. By 1905, the land was formally deeded to Congregation B'nai Israel.

In April of 1885, the following notice appeared in the paper:

The Jewish Society of Butte proposes to erect a synagogue. Three-fourths of the amount required for the building has already been raised and a subscription paper for the balance is being circulated. The site for the new Temple is on the corner of Mercury and Washington Streets, opposite the Catholic Church. It is the determination of the projectors of this enterprise to have the Synagogue completed by the fall of 1885.

The announcement appears to have been a bit premature, because as nearly as can be ascertained, the group mentioned above was the Reform group. Congregation B'nai Israel was not formally organized until August 10, 1897, with William Gallick president, Abraham Wehl, vice-president, and Mose Linz, secretary.

Dr. Morris Eisenberg was the first rabbi of B'nai Israel, and he conducted the High Holy Day services in the Mountain View Episcopal Church. The congregation was formally organized in 1897, and on March 29, 1901, it chose lots on the corner of Washington and Galena streets for its Temple. A religious school was added in 1903. The elegant new building was dedicated on Friday, February 26, 1903, with Rabbi Harry Weiss as spiritual leader. The ladies of the Jewish community organized a ladies auxiliary and Ladies Aid Society, and in November 1906, they formally presented the Temple trustees with $4,250, proceeds from a fair they had sponsored.

Ladies Aid societies flourished in Butte, which had one Reform and one Orthodox women's group. Each had monthly card parties, frequent rummage sales, and other fund-raising activities. A number of Reform and Orthodox members mixed in the Willing Workers, a group that focused on collecting moneys for the victims of European pogroms. B'nai Israel also had an active youth group from about 1904 to 1920, and many Butte Jewish marriages had their beginnings at these club meetings.

Adath Israel, the Orthodox synagogue, was built on Silver Street, across the street from the famous Emma zinc mine. A notice in the Butte *Intermountain* on April 19, 1902, titled "Jewish Residents Buy Synagogue," said:

> *With the payment today of $925, the German Lutheran Church on Silver Street passed into the possession of the Congregation Adath Israel. Within a few months more than $1,000 will be spent on the property in the improvements, making it the first synagogue in Butte, and it is believed, the finest in Montana.*
>
> *Some time ago a part payment was made on the property to bind the bargain. Then the representative Jews of Butte began collecting money for the next payment, that of today. In this work Joseph Weinberg, B. Banks, I. Simon, H. Auerbach, and B. Kopald have been active.*
>
> *Extensive improvements are planned on the church. When it is finished it will be one of the handsomest church edifices in the state.*

By October 1, 1902, Adath Israel was scheduling its initial services in its new building to celebrate the eve of Rosh Hashanah. Services were conducted by I. Simon and Mr. Sabladvosky. They had no rabbi.

Mining weakened the ground beneath the Adath Israel Temple, and by the time of World War I, the Anaconda Company offered to buy the synagogue property so that the entire area could be turned to mining without endangering people. The congregation agreed, then moved to the old Pythian Lodge Hall on South Main for their services. By then, they had Rabbi Ehrlich to lead them. Following Rabbi Ehrlich came Moses Zuckerman, who was both Rabbi and *Shohet*. When the group did not have a resident rabbi, William Canty conducted services. Fire destroyed the Pythian Hall, and the only thing salvaged was the *Sefer Torah*, which had been stored in a small side room of the lodge building.

Controversy was constant within the Orthodox congregation, and at one time it split into three parts. William Meyer was mediator of the melee. In an article entitled "After A Lively Debate Rabbi Chosen," the *Anaconda Standard* reported the following:

> Members of the three Hebrew Orthodox congregations of Butte have weathered a rough sea in efforts put forth the past few weeks to consolidate one large single body under the leadership of one set of officers and one rabbi. However, organization of the combined factions was effected last night and Rabbi Alfred Kahn chosen leader of the flock. It was on the question of extending him a call that the factions were divided and for a time men of the city police department mysteriously appeared upon the scene and quiet was restored.

Two organizations apart from synagogue were important to Butte Jews in particular and Montana Jews in general. The first was the Masonic order. In Montana, Masons dated their place here back to the gold camp of Bannack. On November 12, 1862, when William H. Bell died in that town, he requested a Masonic burial. A notice was posted throughout the mining camp asking all Masons to assemble at a certain log cabin at a certain hour; to everyone's surprise seventy-six members gathered for the funeral service, conducted by Nathaniel P. Langford. The large gathering persuaded the men that they might be able to organize a lodge in Montana, and they received dispensation to do so on June 16, 1863. By that time, however, gold had been discovered in Alder Gulch, the men had scattered, and the idea of an organization was temporarily abandoned. Soon, though, there were lodges established in

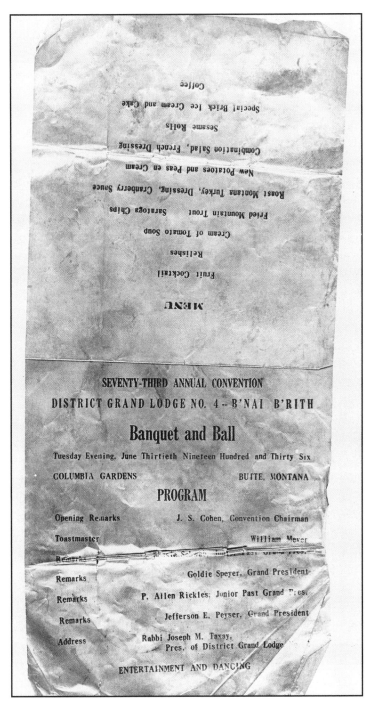

Copper invitation to the B'nai B'rith District Four Grand Lodge 73rd Banquet and Ball, Butte, Montana. COURTESY OF THE LEO SIGMAN FAMILY.

Virginia City and Helena, and on January 24, 1866, a meeting to organize the Montana Grand Lodge of Masons took place. The organization grew rapidly after that, and almost all of the Jewish citizens of the new Montana communities became active Masons, many achieving the highest orders. Butte also had a Masonic lodge.

The other organization important to most Jews of Montana was B'nai B'rith. The only cohesive Judaic group in both Butte and Billings, it was the one medium that promoted social contact between the disparate groups within Butte and between Butte and other Montana towns. Some Montana Jews met for the first time at national B'nai B'rith conventions. Members were drawn from all social and religious factions, and the lodge became the one cohesive factor of the Butte Jewish community. Later, the urge to help fellow Jews caused the community to unite again in their support of the United Jewish Appeal and the Jewish Community Chest. But B'nai B'rith was the Jewish focal point in Butte. The Baron de Hirsch Lodge No. 420, begun in 1892, was the smallest but oldest in the entire district.

Biographical sketches of a few of the early Butte Jews help to paint a picture of Butte. Some early arrivals were miners, but later arrivals were mostly peddlers.

Isador Strasburger, who was born in Russia (Poland) in 1838 came to the United States in 1854. He made his way from New York to Ohio to Kentucky, then crossed the Missouri River. In 1859 he arrived in Denver, Colorado, where he began peddling goods across the country, routing himself through many of the mining communities of the Rocky Mountains. He returned east for a short time, but by May 1863 was one of the first men to arrive in Bannack. Within a month he had set up a tent in the newer boom town of Virginia City, where he operated on the first store in that rough mining center.

The following excerpt from his diary was printed in *The Jewish Archives*:

> *Left Denver early in April [18]63, together with the Kiscadden train. Traveled by Fort Bridger and Soda Springs. Assisted in building the first ferryboat across the Snake River. Thousands of buffaloes crossed our road. Arrived in Bannack July 4 [18]63. Went with the excitement to Alder Gulch. Lived in tent till fall.*
>
> *Had some experiences with George Ives [the bandit]. It was on Sunday. He came in V[irgini]a City [and] demanded a pair of gloves. Not having any, I could not comply with his request. He then drew a six*

shooter, leveled at me and with a S. of a B. and other wild exclamations, coaxed me for the gloves. Being afraid to advance or retreat, I tried to assure him of his waywardness, and with a few more invectives he took an axe that I had as a show and to my utter astonishment, left me unharmed and departed.

A few months later he and others went to where other good Injuns go, to the happy hunting ground, by way of the rope. There were considerable hanging bees in the early times, but as I had witnessed such trifles in [18] 59 and [18]60 at Denver, it did not amuse me any more in V[irgini]a City, and therefore paid no attention to them, but left all the fun for Col. Sanders. Wilbur Fisk Sanders was the scourge of the outlaws.

For twenty years Strasburger remained a successful merchant in Virginia City. But by 1883, as that city began to die, he moved to Bozeman; two years later he went to Butte.

The Virginia City *Tri-Weekly Post* of August 3, 1867, highlighted the marriage of Isador Strasburger to Rachel Cohen, who had been born in New Orleans in 1850 and whose family had moved to Virginia City in 1865. The wedding was performed by "a merchant of the Jewish faith"

Strasburger Store building, Butte. COURTESY OF THE MONTANA HISTORICAL SOCIETY.

and all of the guests, including the governor of Montana and the Secretary of Utah, wore hats, in accordance with Orthodox tradition. Five children were born of this union: Nettie, Eva, Herman (who became Butte City Treasurer), Edgar J. (who became City Engineer and Commissioner of Public Works in Butte), and Rod E. (who worked in mining).

Herman Strasburger was born September 6, 1871, and spent his early life in Virginia City. Graduating from Butte High School, he attended normal school in Deer Lodge. He also studied under private tutors to specialize in bookkeeping, languages (German and French), and mine engineering, and for eighteen months was a law student. Herman started to work at seventeen and had a job in M. P. Sipple Clothing Company, then worked at W. W. Wishon Men's Furnishings establishment, and served for six months as a bookkeeper for David Goldberg in his railroad ticket brokerage. He spent a year in Park City, Utah, then returned to Butte to work with his father in the furniture store. In 1901 Herman Strasburger organized the Safety Fe Company, and he managed the plant for three years. He also ran Pipestone Hot Springs and went into the cattle ranching business. He was elected Butte's city treasurer in 1919. Active in the Masonic order and the Silver Bow Club, he was an officer in several businesses. He married Carrie Lou Lindley in 1906.

Adolph H. (Dolph) Heilbronner was born in Salt Lake City, Utah, on July 6, 1880, to Henry Heilbronner, a native of Bavaria, Germany. The Heilbronner family moved to Butte in 1882 and Henry entered the mercantile business soon after. Dolph attended Butte schools and graduated from Butte High in 1899. Right after graduation he went to work for the Electric Railway Company and became a prime supporter for establishing the Columbia Gardens, a public park and amusement center that became Butte's playground. William Clark, a U. S. senator and one of the "copper kings," financed the venture. Dolph became general agent for the Salt Lake Route, one of Senator Clark's railroads, and he held that position until the federal government took control of the railroad in 1918.

Dolph Heilbronner married Fay Levenson of Portland, Oregon, on October 21, 1907. He and his brother built up a large real estate business, and he developed an expertise in designing advertising campaigns. Dolph promoted the Yellowstone Trail to sell the advantages of Butte, and during World War I he did advertising for the local U. S. Bond drives.

Another Butte man active in advertising was A. A. Sheurman, born in The Dalles, Oregon, January 17, 1886. His German-born father had come to Oregon and had become a buyer of hides and wool. After joining the regular army for a while and participating in some Indian campaigns, he married and settled down. He married Esther Cohn, daughter of M. G. and Emma Cohn of Butte. A. A. Sheurman was one of their two children. Educated in Portland, Oregon, and San Francisco, California, he became a newspaperman and worked for several papers in the Northwest. When he came to Butte in 1909 he specialized in theater advertising. Officed in the Phoenix Building, he was also half owner of the Hippodrome Company, lessee of the People's Theater in Butte, which was built by the Meyer family.

Mr. Sheurman was a member of the Butte Advertising Club, president of the B'nai B'rith Baron de Hirsch Lodge No. 420, and a member of the Elks Club.

David Goldberg became legendary among Butte Jews because of his rise to riches and departure from Butte. Born in Russia on April 12, 1863, David was the oldest of five children. He emigrated to the United States when he was sixteen years old, and worked in his uncle's jewelry business in Cleveland, Ohio, then operated his own business. The lure of the West took him to Salt Lake City, and then to Butte, where he arrived in 1884. Once in Montana, he operated a pawn shop and then a jewelry store until 1890 when he sold out to begin ticket brokering and investing his profits in real estate. Ticket brokering involved buying round-trip tickets at a discount, selling one way tickets to people coming west or going east and pocketing the difference. It was a lucrative business. Goldberg made canny investments in real estate; the Goldberg family, although long gone from Butte, still owns prime property in the city. The family also owns a ranch in western Montana, and David and Minnie's descendants spend vacation time in the state where their grandfather made his initial fortune.

David Goldberg traveled extensively. On one trip, he met Minnie Neuberger of New York; he later married her and decided to settle in that city, changing his family name of Goldberg to Granger and leaving his Jewish roots behind with the old name. The Grangers had two sons: Jeffrey, born in 1891, and Myron, born in 1894. Although he lived in New York and was active in the investment business, David

Granger remained a director of the Silver Bow National Bank and continued to be very active in the Republican Party, which he had strongly endorsed in Montana. He was also a charter member of the Baron de Hirsch Lodge No. 420 of B'nai B'rith.

One of the well-known attorneys in Butte was Mose Seaton Cohen. Cohen was born in Helena to Samuel and Hattie (Silverman) Cohen, who had been the first white people to settle at Choteau, Montana. Samuel Cohen moved to Helena in 1867 where he was in the mercantile business, then moved to Butte in 1895. He had three children: May, born in 1885, who graduated from the New York Conservatory of Music and was a music teacher in Butte; Bert, born in 1884, a Butte insurance man; and Mose, who worked his way through New York Law School, received his Bachelor of Law in 1908, and then settled in Butte to practice law.

Major Julius Silverman, Mose's grandfather, started the first store in Choteau, where he sold merchandise to Indians and white ranchers. Julius's son Samuel was a friend and associate of Colonel Wilbur Fisk Sanders, and he participated in a number of early Montana Indian wars. The family recalled how Grandfather Julius Silverman came from St. Louis, Missouri, in 1858. The journey was made overland by wagon, took six months, and included numerous attacks by hostile Indians. When he was settled, he sent for his wife, Ida, who came to Fort Benton by river from St. Louis, a trip which took three months, and gave her the honor of being one of the first to travel the new river route to Montana. So great was the affection for Julius Silverman, that when Sam Cohen died on August 26, 1920, his wish to be buried next to his father-in-law was honored by the United Hebrew Benevolent Association of Helena.

Another large Jewish family in Butte was the Gallick family. William Gallick, born August 30, 1830, immigrated to the United States when he was twenty years old, landing in New York City in 1850. He settled in New Haven, Connecticut in 1852. There he met and married Blumchen Mandel. The couple decided to move west, traveling to California, to Portland, Oregon, and finally to Montana in 1881. They settled in Butte, where William became a wholesale liquor dealer until he returned east in 1908.

Gallick served as police commissioner and was an active Republican. He served on the reception committee to welcome United States presidents who ventured out west, and in 1908 was chosen to be a presidential elector when William Howard Taft was nominated for president.

Gallick served as president of Temple B'nai Israel for a number of years. He also passed all the chairs of the Ancient Free and Accepted Order of Masons and was a member of a number of other fraternal organizations, including the Baron de Hirsch Chapter of B'nai B'rith, where he was a charter member. His children, all Butte residents, were Mrs. J. G. Sternfels, Mrs. Meyer Genzberger, and Emanuel Gallick.

Jacob Schiffman was the son of a prosperous dealer and exporter of grain and lumber in Zodludek, Russia, where he was born on August 20, 1866. He was educated in Russia until he reached the age of eighteen, at which time he decided to come to the United States. A short stay in New York convinced him that wealth and opportunity lay in the territory of Montana, and within a year he was a resident of Butte.

Schiffman worked in a small store to gain experience and accumulate some capital, then opened his own confectionery store. As early as 1895, he was interested in mining timber and he began supplying mining timber to the Anaconda Company, and also brokering carloads of grain and hay, all the time pursuing other ventures. He built up the confectionery business and sold it in 1901. His imagination was inflamed by stories of other parts of the hemisphere, so he spent his first retirement traveling in Central and South America. Eight months later he came back to Butte to open another confectionery store, which he sold in 1903 to become a traveling salesman for a cigar manufacturer. After one year on the road, he was ready to settle down again; he opened a mercantile store in Gregson Springs, Montana. President Theodore Roosevelt appointed him postmaster of that small community.

Schiffman was a devoted Republican, serving as delegate to the state conventions and prominent in the inner circles of the party. He was one of the directors of the Jewish Charities, a thirty-second degree Mason, a Noble of the Mystic Shrine, and a member of B'nai B'rith. With all of his activities he still found time to become an avid hunter and fisherman.

Schiffman married Nellie Lilburn, a Massachusetts native, in Spokane, Washington, on October 11, 1910. They had one son, Moses, born on September 6, 1911.

Isaac A. Heilbronner was buried in the Butte Jewish cemetery, but his official biography states that his wife was a devout member of the Episcopal Church. This is probably the most graphic picture of Butte's interfaith integration. Heilbronner was born in Salt Lake City on August 2, 1875, the son of Henry and Henrietta Heilbronner, natives of Bavaria, Germany. Henry came to the United States when he was twenty years old, stopped in New York, and then traveled through the Isthmus of Panama to Portland, Oregon. In 1881 he arrived in Butte and entered the furniture business. Henry died in 1884, just three years after his arrival in Butte, but he was able to leave his family a valuable mining interest, which he had acquired on his travels in Carlin, Nevada.

Henry's son Isaac Heilbronner went to school in Butte until he was nine years old, when his mother felt he should have a business education. Hired out as cash boy at the Bonner Mercantile Company, Isaac worked there for the next eight years as cash boy and salesman. After that, he changed employers and became a salesman for Louis D. Cohn, a wholesale cigar manufacturer who started a number of Jewish boys on sales careers.

In 1898, Heilbronner became partners with E. C. Kulli, and they opened a business. He had several partners and several businesses during the next few years, but he eventually sold out and went into mining, incorporating under the name of National Mining and Investment Company in 1906. Several years later the Heilbronner Company was incorporated as a concern devoted to mining brokerage and mining investments.

Heilbronner married Rose Hall, youngest daughter of Captain W. E. Hall, manager of the Alice Mining Company, on February 6, 1900. Captain Hall was the first mayor of Walkerville, a Butte-area community, and politically active in the state. Rose and Isaac's marriage produced one son, Walter Lewis Heilbronner. The Heilbronners were active in the Silver Bow Club, the Butte Country Club, and assorted social organizations. Isaac Heilbronner died on January 4, 1925.

Gus Weinstock, owner of Wein's Clothing Store, arrived in Butte at the age of two, in 1889. Gus was the youngest of five children born to Phillip and Bertha Weinstock. The German-born Weinstock family had traveled as far as Minneapolis when their father, Phillip Weinstock, decided to go west and leave them behind. Phillip made his way to Butte, accompanied by a friend, then sent the friend back to get his family. Phillip Weinstock and Sam Binder opened a slaughterhouse in Butte, but, before long, Weinstock wandered off leaving his five children and their mother to fend for themselves again.

Gus Weinstock left school at age twelve to help support the family. He worked even before his permanent entry into the business world, delivering groceries and liquor after school. His fondest memory of that period was the Christmas he delivered some liquor to William Clark, who was then involved in the election bribery case concerning his election to the United

Gans and Klein store on North Main, Butte, Montana, 1885.
COURTESY OF THE MONTANA HISTORICAL SOCIETY.

States Senate. When Gus delivered the package and handed it to Clark's house boy, he heard Clark say, "Did the delivery boy get his Christmas present yet?" Shortly thereafter, when Gus reported back to his boss, he found a five-dollar gold piece waiting for him, a gift from Clark.

Weinstock worked in a liquor store for a time. As World War I was making headlines, he had opened a grocery store of his own and had married Carrie Oppenheimer. Two things occurred at this time. First, since Carrie came from a family of Reform Jews, for the first time in his life Weinstock got interested in his religion. Second, he received his draft notice and was told to report immediately. He had to close his store almost overnight and sell his merchandise for whatever he could get. Ironically, with the impending flu epidemic and the army red tape, he never served in the army. His biggest personal casualty was the loss of his business.

John Wein had established Wein's Men's Clothing Store in 1907 at 33 East Park Street in uptown Butte. John Wein had many other interests. In 1893 he had patented an improved safety pin, with seven-tenths of the interest assigned to F. A. Fligelman and S. S. Singer of Helena. In 1920, four young men—Gus Weinstock, Ben Meyers, Moe Schwartz, and Harry Gronefine—formed a partnership to turn Wein's into a department store. Schwartz and Gronefine were soon bought out of the four-way partnership and opened Stratford Men's Shop. Weinstock eventually bought out Gronefine, and Weinstock and his family operated the Wein's clothing store well into the twentieth century.

Henry Jonas was an active member of Temple B'nai Israel and B'nai B'rith and was an officer of both. He also gained prominence by being the first citizen of the new state of Montana, since he was first to register as a citizen after the state was admitted to the union in 1889.

Henry's wife invited her sister Renata to visit her in 1898, and the young woman made the trip from Prussia to visit her sister and brother-in-law. At the time of Renata's visit, Butte's Rabbi Morris Eisenberg, who was English, conducted services for the Reform congregation, which was meeting at the Presbyterian Church. Renata was bewildered by the services since she had been brought up in an Orthodox home. The young bride asked Rabbi Eisenberg, a noted Shakespearean scholar, "How do you know what to keep in the services and what to throw out? It is so different from what I am used to."

His answer impressed her, and she related it years later. He said, "If I had a basket of apples, and a couple were rotten, I wouldn't throw out the whole basket. I would choose the good ones and throw the rotten ones away. We've done the same to the services. We have kept the best and thrown out what doesn't belong."

Renata met Abraham Weil during her visit, and marriage resulted. The couple joined the Reform congregation. Abraham had come to the United States from Hamburg in 1884, and by the time they were married, he was established in the rod and gun business. He was also an avid reader and owned a large collection of books. When she was eighty-eight years old, Renata Weil credited her husband with providing her education. "We read and discussed, and everything I know is because of him."

Earle N. Genzburger was born in Helena, the son of Sol and Minnie Israel Genzburger. An accountant, Sol Genzburger was deputy state auditor of Montana from 1898-1900. He had been one of the early Montanans who had journeyed by steamboat in 1878 to Fort Benton and Virginia City before settling in Helena. In 1887, Genzburger was elected vice-president of the Fort Benton Board of Trade. When he finished his state job in Helena, he decided to move to Butte, and for the next thirty-five years he managed the Frank Realty Company. His wife Minnie was also a pioneer; she had arrived in Montana in 1880, traveling by stagecoach from Utah. Their wedding took place in Helena on January 11, 1891.

Earle Genzburger was educated in Helena schools, and then went to the University of Michigan for his college and legal training. He began practicing law in Butte in July 1912, and during World War I he served in the 316th Trench Mortar Battery, 91st division, and with Battery F of the 316th Field Artillery, a unit of the 811st division. Before returning from his overseas assignments, Genzburger spent some time studying at the University of Toulouse, France.

Earle Genzburger became a prominent Butte attorney. The senior member of Genzburger and McGan, a Butte law firm, and an official in several local corporations, he served as president of the Vigilante Council of the Boy Scouts of America, commander of the American Legion (1915-1936), treasurer of Krao Mines, Ltd., treasurer of White's Funeral Home, vice-president of the Greater Butte Mines Corporation, district governor for Kiwanis International (1925), and Grand Chancellor of the Knights of Pythias (1932-1933). From 1950 to 1952 he was Supreme Chancellor and attained the thirty-third degree in the Ancient and Accepted Scottish Rite.

Genzburger was married twice. His first wife, Anna, died in 1925. He later married Karen Knight.

Ed Marens came to Butte as an employee of a firm that sent peddlers west to sell their goods, but was followed by his brothers, Emil and William Canty (the name changed during immigration proceedings). All three brothers came from a small area near Bialystock, Russia. When they arrived in New York, they saw that many of the Jewish immigrants settled together in tenements. Deciding that they would never learn English if they joined their fellow countrymen, and eager to become Americanized as quickly as possible, they recalled a distant relative named I. Simon had settled in Butte, Montana. The brothers made Butte their destination; the arrived in 1912.

William Canty had left a wife and son behind him, and after World War I he had saved enough money to send for his wife and nine-year-old son Avron, who came to Butte in 1921. Young Avron attended the Butte schools during the day, and attended *Chedar* at Moses Zuckerman's butcher shop afterward. Zuckerman was acting rabbi for one of the Orthodox congregations. While teaching his students, his attention would be divided between his butcher trade, his Hebrew students, and the chickens out back, which he killed for his Kosher clientele. When Zuckerman left Butte, lay members took turns reading the Sabbath services. William Canty became the leader of the congregation and conducted services. Avron Canty's *Bar Mitzvah* was celebrated at Adath Israel Congregation on Silver Street when it was still across the street from the Emma mine.

Avron Canty was luckier than most Orthodox children in Butte, since many of them did not receive any formal Jewish education. They generally had a very religious mother or father, lived in a home which kept Kosher, and were imbued with the idea of being "froom," but they did not learn to read or write Hebrew, and they had no Sunday School training. They learned a few of the traditional prayers, insisted on services completely in Hebrew (even though most of them did not understand the language), and kept themselves separate from the Reform Jews of Butte.

Rabbi Ehrlich's name cropped up in interviews of elderly Butte Jews. He was Orthodox, and it is thought he was not really a rabbi, but rather a *Shohet*. He ran a butcher shop for a living, and taught Hebrew in the store while he was working. Many recalled that his store was filthy and that he was dirty about his own person. One of the arguments within the Orthodox congregation occurred because of Ehrlich. A certain group, led by Maurice Meyer, was fed up with Ehrlich's lack of cleanliness and walked out and formed its own congregation. The new group became a bit more conservative, and although they still considered themselves Orthodox, men and women sat together at the services. Ehrlich's group met at the Silver Street synagogue, and Meyer's group met at a rented hall. The second group hired Moses Zuckerman because he promised to keep his butcher shop clean and be more sanitary about the butchering of meat. He carried through with his promise of cleanliness, but then came complaints that he was not doing his own butchering and that his meat was not Kosher. This led to the cessation of trying to keep a Kosher home for many of the Orthodox, for they were without a source of Kosher meat.

Sam Alexander was one of the grand old characters of Butte. A brother of Flora Meyer, he owned the first restaurant in Butte. Alexander was noted for always carrying a large sum of money and for wearing a chain of gold nuggets around his neck and on his watch chain, which drooped across his chest. Sam remained a bachelor and was also a gambler. One day, at the racetrack, he lost a diamond stick pin when a slick robber snipped off his tie just under the knot, enabling him to make off with the pin.

Sam Alexander was known as "Whistlin' Sammy" because he was always whistling the same nameless tune. He claimed he liked the melody, which was his own, and he couldn't understand why people thought he should learn something else. Alexander claimed he had fought in the war against the Nez Perce. He was known to have been in fights in Butte, and one story says that an angry stockbroker threw him down an elevator shaft. He recovered but was never the same. Another story claims he lost the deed to the corner of Montana and Park streets in a poker game. He provided a topic of conversation among people who knew him.

Henry Jacobs was the first mayor of Butte, from 1879 to 1880. He had come to America at age nine and roamed with his family south and west, arriving in Virginia City in 1866. He became a business partner of Leopold Marks in Diamond City, but moved to Butte in 1876 to become one of the first merchants in the mining city. Jacobs's clothing store was chosen as the meeting place for a group planning a vigilante organization similar to the one in Virginia City. Besides serving as mayor, Jacobs became city treasurer,

Henry Jacobs. COURTESY OF THE
MONTANA HISTORICAL SOCIETY.

was a school trustee for three years, and he held other minor offices.
He built the first brick house in Butte and operated a successful clothing
store. Rumors said his death was a suicide, but it was never officially
declared to have been so.

The second Jew in Butte to become
mayor was Henry Lupin Frank, born in Ohio in 1851 to a family that
had its roots in the Alsace region of France. His father was an immigrant
who settled in Cincinnati and became a wholesale merchant there.
After Frank was educated, he set out on his own, living in Colorado
and New Mexico for a couple of years. He came to Butte in 1877. His
first place of business was a log cabin with a dirt roof on Main Street,
but within three years he had moved to larger and sturdier quarters.
He developed mining interests, and was active in politics and fraternal
organizations. In addition to being mayor for two terms, 1885 and
1886, Henry Frank served in the state legislature, from 1889 to 1891,
and was Grand Master of Masons for the state of Montana. An active
Democrat, he attended all Democratic National Conventions and was
a presidential elector in 1886. He was also on the executive board of
the School of Mines in Butte and president of the Butte Water Company.

The Meyer family of Butte became well known throughout Montana. Maurice (born Goodman) Meyer, was a mild-mannered shoemaker; his wife Flora was a shrewd, calculating businesswoman. Her fellow Jews accused her of being miserly, but she managed to invest every penny she could in real estate, and invested wisely. As a result, her children all received fine educations: Helen (Mrs. Meyer Gronfein) and Alice (Mrs. Meyer Schwartz) attended a Jewish girls' school in New York, and William and Harry became lawyers. Sigmund died when he was twenty-one.

William (Billy) Meyer became influential in the Democratic Party. Although he never officially held an elective office, he made and broke many big-time Montana politicians. One of the men he helped to power was Burton K. Wheeler, who in gratitude told many that Meyer was his candidate for a federal judgeship. Everyone assumed that the appointment was a *fait d' accompli*, but Wheeler developed other ideas when he reached Washington. Wheeler was widely know as an anti-Semite after he went to the Capital, and it was an attitude that did not sit well in Butte.

William Meyer was "Mr. B'nai B'rith" to many, and his son Sig Meyer continued the tradition. In 1935, William Meyer, Sig Schilling, Joseph Binnard, and several others, drove to Los Angeles and presented a strong case to make Butte the next B'nai B'rith convention site. Former Butte residents living in Los Angeles joined the delegation in pressing for Butte's selection, and after impassioned speeches by Meyer and Binnard, Butte received the vote. The lodge reached its peak in 1936 when slightly over one hundred members hosted the District Four convention and welcomed members from nine states.

Joseph Binnard was subsequently elected to the executive committee, and in 1939, an unusual precedent was set when Meyer was nominated by his son to the vice-presidency of the Grand Lodge. In 1941, Sig Meyer became president.

The Ehrlichs were one of several other prominent Jewish families in Butte. The Ehrlich family, no relation to the aforementioned *Shohet*, came from eastern Europe, traveled across the plains to Salt Lake City, and then took the day coach to Montana in 1902. The seats on the train were the flush-back style and the windows were kept wide open to get a little fresh air during the torrid summer heat. Still, the heat on the train grew so oppressive it was almost unbearable, and eight little children clutched at their young mother, who did not speak a word of English and was trying not to show how frightened and fatigued she was. She carried oil-cloth bags filled with food for the family and periodically during the long, hot day she would pass out hard-boiled eggs or bread. In the baggage car were all of her cherished possessions, and packed carefully in the midst of them were her dishes, which were her inheritance and her reminder of "the old country." They had all been wrapped individually and packed with loving care, but when she finally arrived in Butte, she found that every dish was smashed! To her, her fortune was lost, because the dishes were a status symbol.

Many years later, one of the Ehrlich children commented wryly on their lives and heritage:

> My dad came with eight kids and two bare hands and a lot of fortitude. He couldn't read or write, and did not know the language, and he didn't have a nickel. He wouldn't have known what to do with it if he had one. I don't know where he got the guts. We'd look around at the Gordons and the other "rich ones." They were the poor people five or six years ahead of us. They were remarkable, these Jews! All across the West are individual Jewish families that came with their packs on their backs and they settled and started businesses, and helped to build the West.

The Gordon family came to Montana from Pennsylvania and Salt Lake City. The father, Mike Gordon, worked in a sweat shop in the East for a dollar a day, and the mother decided they would never get ahead in that fashion. She had an uncle in Carson City, Nevada, so that is where they headed for new opportunities. Mike Gordon went first. On the way west, his train was involved in a bad wreck, and almost all of the passengers were killed. But Gordon managed to jump out of a window and was one of the few survivors. Badly injured, he was hospitalized and got his first taste of western friendliness. People of all backgrounds who had heard of the wreck came to visit him and left money at the hospital to help pay for his care. When he finally recovered, he headed for Salt Lake City to look for a business. Associating himself with another young man, he got a team of horses and began collecting a wagonload of empty five gallon oil cans for salvage. Gordon, in front of the wagon, was bending down to pick up a can when the team bolted out of control and ran away. The two young men were unable to recover their assortment of salvage material, and Gordon was again dead broke.

Eventually, Gordon was able to save enough by doing assorted jobs to bring his wife and children from Pennsylvania where his wife had been supporting the family with her fine sewing. Since Mike had not found financial success in Salt Lake City, the Gordons turned toward Butte and a salvage business in the mining city instead—then expanded their finances to a moderate degree to become the family the Ehrlich children thought was rich in comparison. The Gordon family proliferated; all six children each had five or six children. They all grew up in Butte and attended Butte schools.

When asked what he did as a kid growing up in Butte, Leo Kenoffel answered, "Gambled. This was a gambling town and we learned young."

In Russia, Kenoffel's father heard a visiting American paint a glowing picture of life in the West. He had already put in service in the Russian army, and he was due to be drafted again but a combination of circumstances, including the willingness of the villagers to pool their resources, allowed young Kenoffel to skip over the border and cross the ocean. Once in the U. S., Kenoffel headed for Livingston, Montana, where the Northern Pacific Railroad was hiring men for a dollar a day, a veritable fortune for the young immigrant. More of the Kenoffel family followed, and soon the first-born son was working with his father on the railroad ties during the day and moonlighting at night delivering railroad ties to a baker for fuel. While he was driving a wagon load of the heavy ties, the eldest Kenoffel son had his horse run away; he died in the accident at age seventeen. Saddened by the loss, the Kenoffels decided to leave Livingston and move to Butte, where they became the operators of the Spokane Cafe.

The Kenoffels were a large family. One of the cousins, Barney, was an entertainer and a well known character around Butte. His nickname: "the newsboy mayor."

Several tidbits about the Pincus family: Adolph Pincus made his money in the flophouses and crib properties. Jake Pincus was remembered as the black sheep. "He never did anything right," one of his cronies recalled. "One day a miner came in and offered to trade a mining claim for a gun in Jake's window. Jake needed money, not mining claims, so he turned him down. The mine turned out to be the Mayflower Mine, and William Clark later made millions from it."

Joe Weinberg came to Butte in about 1895. He started selling clothes to prostitutes, selling out of a suitcase. When he made his stake, he opened a fine, ladies ready-to-wear store on West Park next to the Metals Bank. One of his cronies was Louis Rosenstein, a real sport, who had his own ideas about insurance; he would not buy any, even though disasters were always occurring and fire was a constant threat. Rosenstein owned the Empress Theater, which eventually burned down. He did not change his mind about insurance, though—he still would not insure a business. He took his own anti-theft measures. When in the jewelry business, Rosenstein left the store untended. His alarm was a match left hanging on the door latch. If the match was undisturbed when he returned, he knew no one had tried to enter.

The Jewish community in Butte has dwindled over the years and the congregations had to merge in order to survive. From 1897 until 1953 there were rabbis at B'nai Israel, the Reform congregation, and at various times there were Orthodox rabbis employed. Two of the congregations merged in the mid-1960s because of financial constraints, and when that happened one of the ardent Orthodox members refused to set foot in the Temple. Instead he went to Salt Lake City for the High Holy Days.

The zenith of Jewish congregational life in Butte was probably the twenty-fifth anniversary celebration of the dedication of Temple B'nai Israel in the vestry rooms of the Temple on Tuesday evening, February 26, 1929. Thirteen participants in the original dedication services (held in 1904) were present. In 1939, there was the celebration for the thirty-fifth anniversary as well, which grew into a three-day event. On Friday night a community service was held with two Protestant ministers, Rabbi Joseph Gitin, a representative of the congregation, a speaker from the Orthodox congregation, and a public reception. The weekend concluded with a dinner dance at the Finlen Hotel featuring Rabbi Joseph Fink of Spokane, Washington, as guest speaker.

The merger of the Orthodox and the Reform congregations produced a conservative group that used the building at 409 West Park Street that the Orthodox congregation had bought with the money from the Anaconda Company. The remaining Orthodox congregation members were the Cantys, Leo Kenoffel, Kalman Rudolph, the Lusks, the Phil Judds, Anna Rosenberg, Fisher Gordon, Nancy Rafish, Charles Gordon, and Sam Finberg. There were few Reform members left at the time of the merger.

The 1990s have seen a resurgence in Butte's Jewish congregational life with student rabbis in attendance and congregational activities occurring on a regular basis. The emergence of a statewide Jewish organization has been a help in communication between the Jewish communities of the state. In 1994 Congregation B'nai Israel will witness the celebration of its ninetieth anniversary.

CHAPTER THREE

BILLINGS

Montana is so large geographically that there are vast differences between its cities and regions. For instance, Butte and Helena are Rocky Mountain mining towns, but Billings is a trade and oil center for the state's eastern plains. Politically, the mining areas tended to be Democratic because of the influence of the unions; the eastern part of the state has been much more conservative and often votes Republican. Because of the Rocky Mountains bisecting the state, even the weather can differ from east to west. These geographic differences impacted the Jewish community of Billings, which developed in a different way and later than the earlier frontier towns.

Billings is called the Magic City because it developed late in the nineteenth century and "grew like magic." A railroad town, it was the supply center for surrounding irrigated farmland. The establishment of a railroad route made Billings more accessible; its place in the middle of irrigated farmland made it the supply center for thriving agricultural communities in Montana and northern Wyoming. Much of the early capital for Billings investment came from successful ranching operations in the rural region. There was no lure of gold to attract people to this river valley town—until the early 1950s, when oil became to Billings what gold and copper had been to Butte. For a while all the symptoms of a boom economy resulted.

As Billings became a city, it became a place full of churches. Scandanavians and Germans established Lutheran churches there. Catholics of various European backgrounds established a Catholic Church, and a second one also attracted the Mexican population, some of whom were brought in to work the surrounding sugar beet farms. Baptists, Congregationalists, Episcopalians, Presbyterians, and others all built houses of worship. Jews started to filter into the young city around the turn of the century, too. They came mainly from eastern Europe, although some were American born and a few were German born.

Most of the early Billings Jews were very poor, and so intent on making a living that they did not have time to do much about organizing a congregation. Almost all of the Jews who arrived came peddling goods;

some of these were attracted to the hide and fur or salvage business. They were all competitors of one another, since the town could only support so many small, one-man stores or salvage businesses, and this competition tended to restrict their social lives. At first there were barely enough Jewish men for a *Minyon*, which would make a religious gathering "legal." When some of them did get together, there was so much bickering that it resulted in several small groups gathering (instead of one large group) to observe the High Holy Days, although an occasional itinerant scholar or a visiting rabbi might draw them together. The holy days were the only times there were formal religious observances.

The establishment of the B'nai B'rith Lodge No. 815 on June 18, 1917, was an extremely important step toward the establishment of a Jewish community in Billings. The charter was actually granted on July 1, 1917, and the founder and organizer was M. Levy, a merchant who had moved to Billings from Salt Lake City. Charter members of the B'nai B'rith organization were M. Levy, I. T. Zacks, Hyman Lipsker, Ben Zacks, Jacob Miller, Max Friedwald, David Kohn, Sam Fefferman, Louis D. Hoffman, M. Handler, David Barnett, M. Liebman, Max Gerson, Aaron Gordon, Max Rosman, Theodore Schrader, Joe Margolis, Jonathan Levy, Meyer Goldberg, Harry Meister, D. E. Wolfson, Sam Rakow, Abraham L. Hoffman, Manuel Albert, and Louis Litman.

Throughout the first twenty-five years of the organization, there were a total of 160 members. The leadership seemed to pass around and come back again to the same people. A small core of dedicated workers kept the chapter alive and strong. In 1918, after one year of existence, the group's membership had grown to thirty-eight, but by 1931 it had decreased to eighteen. The depression years of 1931 and 1932 were especially difficult for the lodge, and it was often difficult to get a quorum for a meeting. The old standbys—Max Friedwald, Louis Harron, and Alfred Wagner—were always there, and they managed to coerce others into coming to the meetings, which were held twice a month. Many times, the only ones in attendance were the past presidents. The year 1940 saw the group's greatest growth; it counted a membership of sixty. During the following years of World War II, five of the lodge members were in the armed forces: Morris Lipsker, Jerome Wagner, Paul Alweis, Max Frank, and Sam Melnick. Thirty-three of the members lived in Billings, and the remainder stretched across the country, for as people moved away, they still retained their membership in the Billings lodge.

For many years B'nai B'rith meetings were the only link the Jews of

Lodge No. *815* I. O. B. B.

On this *18* day of *June* 19*07* appeared Mr. *Hyman Lipsker* for initiation in *Billings* Lodge, No. *815* I. O. B. B., and having been called upon to answer the questions which would be asked, made the following declaration:

My name is *Hyman Lipsker* I am an Israelite and *21* years old; I was born in *Aug. 15th 1888* I reside *573 N. 35th St. Billings Mont.*; I am by occupation a *Merchant*; I am — married: I pledge obedience to the Constitution, Laws, Rules and regulations of the Independent Order of B'nai B'rith.

I also declare that I have never before been a member of any Lodge of the Independent Order of B'nai B'rith.

Hyme Lipsker

WITNESS,

J. Backer Secretary.

On this *18th* day of *June* 19*07* appeared Mr. *Jacob Miller* for initiation in *Billings* Lodge, No. *815* I. O. B. B., and having been called upon to answer the questions which would be asked, made the following declaration:

My name is *Jacob Miller* I am an Israelite and *54* years old; I was born in *Oct. 15th 1862* I reside at *Billings Mont. 7421 Monterey ave*; I am by occupation a *Merchant*; I am — married: I pledge obedience to the Constitution, Laws, Rules and regulations of the Independent Order of B'nai B'rith.

I also declare that I have never before been a member of any Lodge of the Independent Order of B'nai B'rith.

Jacob Mill

WITNESS,

J. Backer Secretary.

37

Lodge No. I. O. B. B.

33

On this *11th* day of *Sept* 19*07* appeared Mr. *Otto Werner* for initiation in *Billings* Lodge, No. *815* I. O. B. B., and having been called upon to answer the questions which would be asked, made the following declaration:

My name is *Otto Werner* I am an Israelite and *40* years old; I was born in *March 17th 1877* I reside *at Billings Mont.*; I am by occupation a *Hide Buyer*; I am — married: I pledge obedience to the Constitution, Laws, Rules and regulations of the Independent Order of B'nai B'rith.

I also declare that I have never before been a member of any Lodge of the Independent Order of B'nai B'rith.

Otto Werner

WITNESS,

J. Backer Secretary.

On this *11th* day of *Sept* 19*07* appeared Mr. *Louis Harron* for initiation in *Billings* Lodge, No. *815* I. O. B. B., and having been called upon to answer the questions which would be asked, made the following declaration:

My name is *Louis Werner* I am an Israelite and *39* years old; I was born in *Nov. 29. 1876* I reside *at Billings Mont.*; I am by occupation a *Hide Dealer*; I am *not* married: I pledge obedience to the Constitution, Laws, Rules and regulations of the Independent Order of B'nai B'rith.

I also declare that I have never before been a member of any Lodge of the Independent Order of B'nai B'rith.

L. Harron

WITNESS,

J. Backer Secretary.

Pages from the records for I.O.O.B. (B'nai B'rith) Lodge Number 815 in Billings, Montana.
COURTESY OF CONGREGATION BETH AARON.

Billings had with one another. The community would turn out when a grand lodge officer visited Billings, or would come together for Rosh Hashanah and Yom Kippur. The early meetings were held at the Odd Fellows Hall; later they were held at the Knights of Pythias Hall in the Stapleton Building. The lodge contributed three hundred dollars to the building fund for the new temple which was built in 1940, and after the building was completed, they held their meetings in the basement of the Temple. Meetings were extremely brief because the members were eager to adjourn to the pinochle table. Members of the Billings lodge remember acrimonious meetings where members vented their hard feelings to one another about a myriad of petty problems. The organization finally put an official stop to the bickering that had become so frequent by adopting a rule that personal grievances could not be aired at lodge meetings.

Having an active B'nai B'rith organization was not organization enough for a growing Jewish community. During the flu epidemic of 1918, the Jewish residents of Billings realized that they needed a cemetery. They had been sending their burials to Butte, which finally suggested they establish their own burial grounds. In order to raise money for the land, an auction was held, giving the highest bidder the right to name the cemetery and the congregation that would be formed to maintain it. Louis Harron won the bid, and chose the name Beth Aaron, a translation of his name.

Friday night religious services for the Beth Aaron congregation began in the 1930s when three women—Mrs. Dan Kohn, Aurice Solomon (a converted Jewess), and Mrs. Dave Werner—started to hold services in their homes. Prior to the building of the Temple, the women would occasionally get together for a bridge game, as well, and for awhile they had a sewing club. Soon, however, the younger women decided to split off in a separate group, and a social chasm erupted which lasted for many years. But men trickled into the services, and the women persuaded them to try to raise money for a sanctuary. Among the first donors were Louis Harron, Arthur and Dave Werner, Hyme Lipsker, Louis Melnick, Alfred Wagner, Simon Sigman, Sam and Jake Letwak, George Sukin, Sid Cohn, Frieda Kohn, Sam Werner, Morris, Herb and Pete Werner, and Ollie Koppe. Dave Werner donated the Ark, the candlelights, and paid off the balance of the small mortgage. The building, at 1148 N. Broadway, was completed in 1940, and was formally dedicated as Temple Beth Aaron by Israel Friedman of Denver.

Louis Harron led a movement to have men and women worship together at Temple Beth Aaron rather than sit apart in the Orthodox tradition. Volunteers took turns leading the services. It was another decade before a rabbi was hired, and not until 1953 was the decision made to affiliate with the Union of American Hebrew Congregations, the Reform arm of American Jewry. With membership in the national organization, an ordained Reform rabbi became a reality for the Billings congregation.

As the aforementioned petty grievances indicate, Billings was not the open society that Helena and Butte were in their early days. Infighting within the community was just a reflection of the Billings community in general. Anti-Semitism was manifested early, so Jews generally did not try to mingle with their non-Jew neighbors. During the 1920s, the growth of the Ku Klux Klan augmented the animosities. Members of the Klan infiltrated the Masonic order in Billings, and for a period of ten years no Jews were admitted to that organization. During the 1920s, both Jewish and Catholic merchants felt the sting of an economic boycott orchestrated by the Klan, and it was fifty years before either Jews or Catholics were elected to the school board. Jews were not admitted to the Hilands Golf Club and in the early days of the Junior League, Jews were not invited to join. This spirit lasted into the 1950s and 1960s; I was told by friends who were Junior League members that the anti-Semitism was a rule of the national organization. The rule changed, locally anyway, in the 1970s.

The post-World War II era brought many young Jewish families to

Temple Beth Aaron, Billings, Montana, June 1965. COURTESY OF CONGREGATION BETH AARON.

Montana and especially to Billings. Many of the new arrivals were college educated or veterans who were looking for business opportunities. The discovery of oil in the Williston Basin in the beginning of the 1950s created a boom town in Billings. Although the oil finds were to the east and north of the Yellowstone River valley, Billings drew many geologists, attorneys, real estate agents, and representatives of major oil companies who established their offices here and brought their families to live in the city. This rapid influx of oil people attracted merchandisers, salespeople, and professionals who spotted opportunities in the city as well. For them, Billings was perfectly located as a marketing center because of its accessibility to rail and air transportation.

The Jewish community grew from all of this activity, as did the rest of the population. By 1951 Congregation Beth Aaron had hired a full-time rabbi, Rabbi Belton. However, because the congregation had so little experience with an organized congregation and a full-time rabbi, there was controversy about Rabbi Belton's abilities, and he stayed less than a year. The religious services at Beth Aaron were a curious blend of Orthodox, Conservative, and Reform styles, because of the mixed backgrounds of the congregation. For instance, the Reform prayer book was used on Friday nights; the Conservative prayer book was used on all religious holidays. Men wore hats during services, but men and women sat together. No one kept a Kosher home, and the services were expected to be quick so that the men could adjourn to the basement for their weekly poker game, and the women could play bridge.

By 1952, because of the number of new young Jewish families in Billings, there were nearly one hundred children who needed religious education. Rabbi Moishe Maggal was hired to direct the congregation and its Sunday School. He lasted two years. Again the congregation was divided about what they expected from him, and there were doubts raised about whether he was really a rabbi. Congregation meetings were held after Friday night services; the meetings devoted to the question of contract renewal got so heated that verbal abuse became commonplace and meetings often lasted until well after midnight. For those newcomers who had moved from large cities and established congregations, the situation was unbelievable.

One advance made during Rabbi Maggal's tenure was the creation of a choir, led by Rachel Maggal, the rabbi's young wife. The addition of music to the services added more solemnity to the Sabbath, and the choir members, wearing black robes and accompanied at the piano by Frieda

Temple Beth Aaron 1945 confirmation class. Left to right: Louis Melnick, Charles Wayman, Buddy Sukin, Cookie Bernstein, Dorothy Cohen, Ruth Werner, Arnold Stone, Mr. Friedman. COURTESY OF CONGREGATION BETH AARON.

Letwak, were much appreciated. But Rabbi Maggal's contract was not renewed in 1954, when the congregation decided to affiliate with the Union of American Hebrew Congregations and try to hire an ordained Reform rabbi. Rabbi and Mrs. Samuel Horowitz accepted the pulpit in 1954, and remained in the position for twenty-five years.

Rabbi Horowitz had been ordained in 1931 and had served in pulpits in Pennsylvania, Wisconsin, Kansas, and Washington before arriving in Billings. After serving as chaplain during World War II in the China-Burma-India theater of war, on June 15, 1962, he received an honorary doctorate of divinity from the Hebrew Union College-Jewish Institute of Religion. In Billings he served on the mayor's committee on urban renewal, the Governor's committee on domestic relations, and numerous other boards. Rabbi Horowitz joined the Ministerial Association and became active in it. Brotherhood Week became a community wide action, and churches were invited to come to services and learn about their Jewish neighbors. At Chanukah, the Jewish children shared their holiday with their public-school friends by explaining why they celebrated Chanukah and what the symbols meant. Many of the churches began to have model Seders on Passover so they could teach their congregations about the holiday. Rabbi and Mrs. Horowitz and many of the others in the congregation were invited to help their neighbors learn about the holiday. Boy Scout and Girl Scout troops with Jewish and non-Jewish members shared joint celebrations.

Minna Horowitz began to work at St. Vincent Hospital, which is directly across the street from the Temple, and as Rabbi Horowitz was engaging in interfaith activities in the community, Minna became part of the Catholic Hospital. One Friday night, to everyone's delight, nuns and a priest were welcomed to their first visit to a Jewish Temple. The Horowitzes were responsible for a change in attitude about mingling with the entire community.

Within the Beth Aaron congregation, Rabbi Horowitz taught Hebrew to the children and prepared both boys and girls for Bar and Bat Mitzvah. In addition to the Hebrew School, there was an active Sunday School with parents acting as teachers and administrators, and materials provided by the Union. A confirmation class taught jointly by Dr. Aaron Small and Julie Brown (Coleman) concentrated on the history of religion. Each Sunday, as the class of five learned about a religion, they attended that particular church, so that the students could experience firsthand what they were learning. A children's choir was added to the activities, led by Minna Horowitz and accompanied by Betty Kohn. In order for the children to learn to be proud of their own traditions, the Sunday School committee held decoration contests for the children of the Sunday School. Parents and children were urged to decorate their homes for Chanukah, just as their gentile neighbors decorated for Christmas, and a committee visited every home they were invited to and gave little prizes. Blue and white lights, menorahs in windows, and Stars of David in the homes all added to the celebration, and the children were urged to value their traditions instead of trying to copy their non-Jewish friends.

Sponsored by the Jewish Chautauqua Society, Rabbi Horowitz became a "flying rabbi." He taught religious school Sunday mornings, boarded a plane and flew to Missoula where he taught classes in religion at the University of Montana on Mondays and Tuesdays, then flew back to Billings Tuesday nights. He also went to the Great Falls Air Force base frequently, and whenever there was a need for a rabbi in the state he was called. When Rabbi Horowitz retired, he and his wife Minna remained in Billings, since the community had become home to them.

There were so many young Jewish children in the Beth Aaron congregation in the early 1950s that there was serious talk about expanding the building to have room for religious school classes. Members eyed the house next door for possible expansion, but prudently decided to make do with the space they had. They divided the basement with ceiling to floor curtains on adjustable rods, so there could be four classrooms plus one in the cloakroom. One class was held in the sanctuary, and one in the rabbi's office. The building seemed to be bursting at the seams, but as that "baby boom" generation grew up there was never again that demand for school space. The only other times that space became a problem was at Rosh Hashanah and Yom Kippur. Not only did all of the Billings people show up for services, but there were regulars from Glendive, Lewistown, Miles City, and other towns in Montana and Wyoming. Often there were so many chairs squeezed into the sanctuary that there was worry about fire codes.

Among the parents of the burgeoning Sunday School population in the mid-1950s were Ed and Helen Feldman, Ed and Ruth Bernstein, Aaron and Lil Lipsker, Morrie and Zella Nemer, Leonard and Florence Gordon, Aaron and Gerry Moyer, Mel and Julie Brown (Coleman), Reuben and Florence Bresky, Jack and Rose Lutzker, Jake and Frieda Letwak, Morrie and Yetta Niss, Art and Betty Meyer, Jerry and Betty Kohn, Max and Claire Buman, Herb and Ruth Werner, Arnie and Sylvie Baron, Aaron and Beverly

Temple Beth Aaron junior choir, 1958. COURTESY OF CONGREGATION BETH AARON.

Small, Shorty and Gretchen Alterowitz, Leo and Rosa Sigman, Harry and Ceil Anisgard, Joe and Helen Sukin, Sam and Sue Melnick, Harry and Kitty Mitzman, Jack and Louise Vinner, Jack and Frieda Kleinrok, Dave and Dena Wigodsky, Bud and Emma Morgan, Albert and Rose Berlant, Perry and Karen Berg, Hans and Marge Rossen, Sam and Jeanette Werner, and Marian Meyer.

By 1955, the active parent group decided to have a summer camp at Red Lodge, so Camp Beth Aaron was born. The camp was held on the leased campgrounds of the Lions Camp. Goldie Stone volunteered to be camp cook; Shorty and Gretchen Alterowitz, Rabbi and Minna Horowitz, Leonard Gordon, and others became counselors. Worship services were held under the stars, and a busy program of arts and crafts, physical activities, religious studies, and music was incorporated into the week-long program. The camp continued yearly until 1958.

During the active 1950s there were also elaborate *Oneg Shabbats* served after Friday night services, and a big party was held after breaking the fast on Yom Kippur. Recorded music was provided as dance music, and the event was attended by those of all ages. At Passover, a community *Seder* became a tradition on the second night of Passover. It was held in the basement of the Temple until space became a premium and it was moved to a hotel. Still later it moved to Eastern Montana College. In 1993 the Temple basement was filled to capacity. That year, Al Small

Sabbath service, Camp Beth-Aaron, Red Lodge, Montana, 1955. COURTESY OF CONGREGATION BETH AARON.

75

Billings Gazette

SECTION THREE

Tuesday Morning, September 19—15 H '72

"Yom Kippur begins on traditional note," September 19, 1972. COURTESY OF THE BILLINGS GAZETTE.

served as chief cook and chairman, and Student Rabbi Jon Davidson presided.

After Rabbi Horowitz retired, a pattern emerged: the congregation obtained student rabbis who flew in bi-weekly from Cincinnati, and at different times had two full-time rabbis. The first full-time rabbi after Rabbi Horowitz was Rabbi Kenneth Ehrlich, who was in Billings two years then heeded a call to become the Dean of the Hebrew Union College-Jewish Institute of Religion in Cincinnati. Several years of student rabbis ensued until Rabbi Robert Ratner was hired; he stayed in Billings for three years. The congregation began to grow smaller during Rabbi Ratner's tenure. With costs escalating, the congregation felt they could no longer afford a full-time rabbi, so Rabbi Ratner's contract was not renewed.

Two student rabbis have served since Rabbi Ratner moved east to serve another congregation. Services are held every Friday night, with the interim weeks handled by lay leaders. Hebrew School is taught by the student rabbis on the alternate weeks they are in Billings, and their weekend stay is augmented with adult study groups, adult Hebrew classes, and youth group events.

Congregation Beth Aaron remains a viable presence in the Billings community, and its members now participate widely in community affairs. The establishment of the Yellowstone Country Club after World War II provided an opportunity for golfers to belong to a country club, no matter their religion. Young Jewish matrons have been invited to join the Junior League, and a number of members of the Beth Aaron congregation have served on boards of philanthropic organizations and have been active politically. Rabbi Ehrlich and Rabbi Ratner taught classes at Eastern Montana College in Billings under the sponsorship of the Judaic Studies grants, and were well received.

The reappearance of the Ku Klux Klan in the 1990s in Billings has brought a different response than it did earlier in the century. A marked surge in hate activities occurred in 1993. At Rosh Hashanah, vandals turned over most of the headstones in the Jewish cemetery at that holy time and as a long-time member of the community was being buried. The threats are reminders of the Klan's hatred, but this time there has been widespread community support and outrage at the vandalism and

Sabbath service at Temple Beth Aaron Temple, 1993, with cantor Samuel M. Cohon.
COURTESY OF THE AUTHOR.

threats against Jewish people. After the *Billings Gazette* printed the story and pictures and television news showed the damage, help was immediately offered to repair the damage. Shortly thereafter, when there was a bomb threat made to the congregation during the High Holy Day services, an armed guard had to be employed to guard the building as the congregation came in to worship. Again, there was community support.

Chanukah brought more outrages. Rocks were thrown into windows of two homes, barely missing small Jewish children, and hate messages accompanied the acts. Since then, there have been pamphlets circulated maligning Jewish members of the community as well as Jews in general. A strong Human Rights Commission in Billings and an enlightened newspaper spotlighted these terrible events, and community outrage resulted in a candlelight vigil by the general citizenry the night of Chanukah services. The paper printed full-page menorahs and asked readers to post them in their windows to show support for the ideas of peace and unity. Many churches and individuals joined in putting menorahs in their windows—and unfortunately found themselves targets of the same bigots who had been harassing the Jewish community. The First Methodist Church had several of its windows broken, and a number of cars were battered because of their owners' sympathies with Jews. The Beth Aaron congregation, meeting to discuss the above events, felt that the acts were those of a small group, and that the overwhelming friendship

Jewish cemetery, Billings. COURTESY OF THE AUTHOR.

Vandals attack churches

Gazette photos by James Woodcock

Scattered light falls on Pastor Tim Hathaway after vandals shattered the glass door to the Evangelical United Methodist Church. A menorah was displayed beside the door.

Windows with menorahs broken by rock throwers

■ **Hate crimes:** Chief urges public to express outrage

By GREG McCRACKEN
Of The Gazette Staff

Two Billings churches and six West End homes, all bearing the images of menorahs in their windows, were vandalized in the past several days, apparently by hate groups, according to law enforcement officers.

"What the hate groups would have us do is not publicize and not express our outrage," Billings Police Chief Wayne Inman said Wednesday. "They would have us be silent and we can't agree to be silent. We have to agree to be more vocal in our opposition."

Paper reproductions of menorahs graced either side of the glass doors at Evangelical United Methodist Church, 345 Broadwater Ave. Late Tuesday or early Wednesday, vandals shattered the door.

At the First United Methodist Church, 2800 Fourth Ave. N., copies of menorahs were hung in each of the windows. Bricks or stones were thrown through two of the windows, with one stone aimed directly at the menorah, said Cathie Pasco, administrative secretary.

"We're not going to take them out; we need to leave the menorahs in," she said. "We're still supporting our Jewish brothers and sisters. That's our heritage and I know they appreciate that."

According to Yellowstone County Sheriff Chuck Maxwell, five Yellowstone Country Club homes and another residence located on the West End all had vehicles damaged early Sunday. Each home carried a paper reproduction of a menorah in a window.

Linda Marshall, diaconal minister at First United Methodist Church, said a menorah at her church took a "direct hit."

66 We're not going to take them out; we need to leave the menorahs in."
— Cathie Pasco
church secretary

Maxwell said two of the families received late-night telephone calls from the vandals, who made derogatory remarks about Jews before telling the owners to go out and look at their vehicles. Cars in front of all six homes were stomped on and had windows kicked out.

Inman said that despite the vandalism apparently targeted at people with menorahs in their windows, the community must not give in to hate groups.

"Visible signs of support for the Jewish community have to increase and not decrease," he said. "For every vandalism that is made, I hope that 10 other people put menorahs in their windows."

Sarah Anthony, president of the Billings Human Rights Coalition, expressed her outrage.

"When you offend one member of the community, you offend us all, and you answer to all of us," she said.

In Saturday's issue, The Billings Gazette printed a reproduction of a menorah and urged all citizens to display the menorah in their doors or windows to "let all the world know that the irrational hatred of a few cannot destroy" what people in Billings and the United States have built. The move came after vandals on Dec. 2 threw a brick through the window of a Billings Jewish home.

(More on Crimes, Page 15A)

"Windows with menorahs broken by rock throwers,"
December 1993. COURTESY OF THE BILLINGS GAZETTE.

shown by the majority of the Billings community was indeed a welcome change from the cooler climate of earlier years.

In order to look at the lives of Billings-area Jews over the decades and watch the development of the local Jewish community, we will again turn to certain strong individuals as examples.

One of the first Jews to arrive in Billings was Sam Fefferman. Born in Poduloesky, Russia, on September 23, 1885, Fefferman came to America with his widowed mother in 1897. They went to Minneapolis where at the age of twelve he peddled papers and went to night school to learn English. By the time he was sixteen, Fefferman was ready for business, so he entered the hide and fur trade. He worked for Minneapolis furriers Gordon and Ferguson for a year, and then in 1902 decided to move to Billings, Montana. Starting on a very small scale, he began to deal in hides, fur, wool, and metal, buying and selling whatever he could. He ranged over eight hundred miles in his business route, using Billings as a home base. Eventually he was able to open a store at 25th and Minnesota Avenue; he lived at 707 North 25th Street.

Louis Harron with his hide wagon, about 1910. COURTESY OF SAM MELNICK.

For a short time, there were three Fefferman brothers in Billings: Sam, Adolph, and Morris. Each brother married one of three sisters who lived in the city, the Samuels girls, who had also come from Russia. Adolph's daughter was Frieda, who married Hyme Lipsker.

In 1904, Louis Harron arrived in Billings, on Montana's passing frontier. Born in Kalwarje, Lithuania, on September 29, 1876, Harron made travels that took him to Washington, D.C.; Pittsburgh, Pennsylvania; Denver and Cripple Creek, Colorado; and Butte, Montana. When he at last arrived in Billings, he found three Jewish families and a couple of bachelors had arrived before him.

Harron became the backbone of the Billings Jewish community. When Temple Beth Aaron was built, Harron's contributions earned him the right

to have the congregation named after him. Congregation Beth Aaron was the translation made of his name. A perennial bachelor, he was known as a roué around the state, and his friends claimed he had a girlfriend in every town he visited. He began as a horse and wagon peddler and worked around eastern Montana, and he eventually saved enough to become the owner of an auto parts business that became successful enough for him to leave a sizable legacy to his beloved congregation and to some of "his congregation children."

Louis Harron Night became a yearly celebration for Beth Aaron members; it is still celebrated in the 1990s. The following tribute was composed by Sam Melnick in Harron's honor while he was still alive:

Friends, we are gathered here tonight to honor a little man who has been protruding in front for the past five or six years He wears

Louis Harron in 1935. COURTESY OF SAM MELNICK.

Louis Melnick, Hyman Harron, and Louis Harron in Yellowstone National Park, 1920.
COURTESY OF SAM MELNICK.

brown oxfords in the summer and high brown shoes in the winter. He owns a bright shiny Plymouth, tan in color, with an old-time shift gear. Shortly after he bought the car he received a letter from the president of Chrysler Corp thanking of him for buying the very last Plymouth with a floor gear shift. Of late, he has developed a marked talent for cookery. He would appreciate a Maxwell Settlement cookbook. He isn't a fancy cook, but he makes a wicked stew. He despises celery, lettuce, and greens of all kinds. He likes well seasoned pickles, and if he were a married woman, that might be an indication of something!

He must have water with all his meals. In dancing, he shakes all over. In his younger days (a matter of six or seven years ago!) he could outdance any man his junior, but now, we don't know. He is very methodical, slow, cautious, and cannot be rushed, not even into marriage! His pet defense phrase, when anyone tries to hurry him is: Don't rush me. Almost every move he makes is usually planned, cogitated and debated beforehand. His campaign of mailing Christmas cards, New Year's cards and Rosh Hashanah cards has only been matched by that of General Eisenhower on D Day.

He fears for a flood pouring over the curb of 12th Avenue, into the basement of this center. He has a phobia about the frigidaire in the center catching fire if it is connected, particularly when no one is in the center. He worries and stews about cigarette smoke getting into the upper hall of the center.

We believe he has travelled to Washington, D.C., four times to see the late President Roosevelt inaugurated.

By this time it has probably dawned upon you and upon him that we are referring to Louis Harron, our shamus and the strongest pillar of our community, our congregation and our Lodge. Most of us here assembled have not given much thought to the valuable service he has rendered the community. We have accepted it as though it was part of our breathing. Going back to the time before the center was built when pledges were being taken to build this building, Harron donated the largest amount. He promised this donation only on condition that no mortgages be placed on the center. When he was informed it could not be built without a mortgage, without a murmur, he released the congregation from its promise. This was an indication of his willingness to cooperate at all times.

It is very seldom that a community is blessed like we have been blessed with an individual like Louie Harron. It isn't very difficult for most of us to recall incidents where Harron has gone off the beaten path to render some service or courtesy to us individually. The small incident, for instance, of putting his car at the disposal of some local servicemen on furlough. He has a particular fondness for the young people of our community. If he had his way, none of the younger people would ever pay a penny of dues or charge of any kind. The care he has given this building is known to all of us. The services he has rendered the community cannot be paid in dollars and cents.

In recognition of all this, Louie, we are presenting to you a small token of affection to a fine man of sterling character. May it give you as much pleasure and satisfaction in its use as it has given all of us in bestowing it upon you. But what is of more value to you is the esteem and good will we bear you. May you be with us for many years to come, for no one can ever take your place in our hearts.

Harron was a devoted member of B'nai B'rith, and he rarely missed a convention. Sig Meyer of Butte recalled fondly that the year he was elected grand president, Louis Harron became his self-appointed campaign manager. But Harron never caught on to the fact that many of the people he was introducing Sig to, and many of the votes he thought he was gathering, were people that were long-time acquaintances of the Meyer family. He was so enthusiastic about Montana, and anyone who lived in Montana, that despite his small stature, his bright blue eyes and grin would captivate those he buttonholed as he boosted his state's candidate for the high lodge office.

After Harron's death in 1959, his attorneys sent a letter to Louis Melnick, Sam Melnick, and Leo Sigman regarding the Louis Harron Trust:

> Gentlemen:
>
> For the purposes of clarifying your position as trustees of Lot 4, Block 109, Original Town of Billings, under the testamentary trust set forth in the Last Will and Testament of Louis Harron deceased, I would like to quote certain pertinent sections of the testamentary trust, together with certain pertinent sections of our law relating to such trust.
>
> The pertinent sections of the Last Will and Testament pertaining to the trust are as follows:
>
> "I give, devise, and bequeath to Louis Melnick, Sam Melnick, and Leo Sigman, that certain real estate...in trust, however, for the following purposes: The net income from said property shall be used by said trustees for the benefit, upkeep and maintenance of Beth Aaron Cemetery, situated west of Billings, Yellowstone County, Montana, and of the Jewish Center and Beth Aaron Temple, located at 12th and 28th Street, Billings, Montana. I hereby direct said trustees to divide and use the net income from said property between the cemetery and said Center and Temple in such amounts as their judgement dictates is necessary for support of maintenance of said cemetery, Center and Temple...In all matters effecting the management, control and disposition of the aforesaid trust estate, a decision of the majority of trustees shall be controlling. In the event of the resignation, disability or death of all of the aforesaid trustees, I hereby appoint as alternate trustee, Montana National Bank of Billings, Montana . . . "

Louis Harron's devotion to his congregation remains a constant, years after his death.

The name Lipsker was a familiar one in the Billings Jewish community for over sixty years. Aaron Lipsker was the first of the Lipsker family to arrive in the city and he opened a small store.

Soon his brother Hyme Lipsker arrived from Romania to join him in work. Hyme became his brother's heir, and being a good merchant and a shrewd businessman, he used his inheritance to build what became the Popular Store. On the corner of Montana and 27th streets, across the street from a jeweler, the store carried men's and ladies' clothing. The store prospered, but Hyme could foresee the eventual decline of Montana Avenue as the premier shopping street. He sold his store, but not before he invested in real estate. The Lipskers owned a variety of properties, including the Babcock Building, which still occupies the main corner of the downtown business section at Broadway and Second Avenue North.

Hyme Lipsker married Frieda Fefferman and they became the parents of three children: Morris, Aaron, and Ruth. Frieda Lipsker had a broad smile that captivated all who knew her. She would walk down the street and greet everyone she met. Since she had come to Billings as a bride in 1908, she seemed to know everyone; as the Lipsker fortune grew, Frieda remained a friend to all. As a widow, she became one of the financial mainstays of the Beth Aaron congregation. In 1960, the congregation surprised her with a testimonial dinner; seventy-five guests attended. Frieda died prematurely on August 7, 1965. Her funeral had standing room only, as people from all walks of life crowded into Michelotti-Sawyers Mortuary to bid her good-bye.

Contemporaries of Hyme Lipsker, who preceded Frieda in death, claimed that when he wanted a job done, he purposely did not get bids for the job, but instead rounded up workmen, told them what to do, then argued the price. By the 1930s, the Lipskers were numbered among the wealthy in Billings. They wintered in Florida, and Hyme, Frieda, and their daughter Ruth traveled to Europe for an extended visit. Their older son Morris attended Shattuck Military Academy; Aaron graduated from Northwestern University in Chicago, where he met his wife Lillian, and earned a Master's Degree from the University of Colorado; and Ruth attended Northwestern University, where she met and subsequently married her husband, Dr. Bertram Moss.

Temple Beth Aaron was in the planning stages while Hyme Lipsker was in Florida one year. Loath to let anyone else direct the project, he kept a series of communiques coming from Florida. He consulted a Florida architect, who knew nothing about Montana and the small community of Billings, and had him draw up plans. The result called for a grandiose structure, much too large for the small group of thirty families who were supporting the venture. Part of a letter sent back to Billings by Lipsker

Dinner honoring Frieda Lipsker, at Temple Beth Aaron, Billings, 1960. Left to right:
Lillian Lipsker, Rabbi Horowitz, Frieda Lipsker, Minna Horowitz, Aaron Lipsker.
COURTESY OF CONGREGATION BETH AARON.

read:

> *See Melnick and tell him to give me the size of the windows and*
> *how many he will need as I can get them wholesale and they look*
> *much better than wood. Also if he a got a letter from the man in*
> *Miami Beach the scetsh and tell him not to let the contract go until I*
> *get home. They have plenty of time as long as I am in it I want it built*
> *right so they can wait for me. It is a long time until fall yet.*

Despite the pressure from Lipsker to build the building his way, it
was erected according to specifications drawn up by a Billings contrac-
tor. For many years afterward, Hyme Lipsker refused to set foot inside.
Ruth Lipsker Moss said of her high school days in Billings:

> *I was so glad when the High Holidays fell on Sunday and I could*
> *say I was going to church, too. I had no Jewish friends my age, and I*
> *was very conscious of my religion because of my parents. When other*
> *kids were going to church or church related activities, I felt completely*
> *outside. I didn't know what it meant to belong to a group until I went*
> *away to college.*

Morris Lipsker came back from service in World War II and bought
Chapple's Drugs, which was located on the corner of Broadway and
Montana Avenue next to the Northern Hotel. It was an active place in the

early 1950s, because the Northern Hotel bar was a meeting place for many of the oil promoters, speculators, and investors, and Chapple's Drugs was right down the street. In his middle age, Morris Lipsker married a Mexican woman who died in childbirth, leaving him with a daughter, Louise. Grief-stricken by his loss, he ignored the child and moved to Mexico. The child was raised by her mother's sister, Lena, although while Morris's mother Frieda was alive she doted on the child and often could be seen walking down Broadway pushing the baby's carriage.

Aaron Lipsker and his wife Lil were very much a part of the Billings congregation and community. The Aaron Lipskers operated a sporting goods store, Q's, from 1953 until they left Billings in 1962. Aaron's main activities were managing the family properties and playing duplicate bridge; he was one of the first Life Masters in the community. Aaron and Lillian had four children: Barry, Scott, Hylan, and Shana. They moved to California after Frieda Lipsker's death and severed their connection to Billings. Aaron and his son Barry died within the same year, 1993, in Olympia, Washington, where Lil, her son Scott, and his family still live in 1994.

The Werner family played a prominent role in the early Billings community. Ben Werner came to the Billings area in the 1890s, living and working from a horse and wagon. He saved his money and left the area, moving to Chicago where he managed to become a veterinarian. His brother Arthur emigrated from Odessa, Russia, to Milwaukee, Wisconsin, where most of his children were born. He then moved to Montana, shortly after the turn of the century. He became a hide buyer, and when he had settled and made a few dollars, he sent for his wife and seven children: Morris, Pete, Israel, Samuel, Herbert, Dave, and a daughter who died young. For a brief time Arthur Werner and Louis Harron were partners, with Harron working the Big Timber area and Werner working the Billings area. But by the end of World War I, Harron had settled in Billings and opened his own business.

The Arthur Werners and their seven children struggled to survive, but Mrs. Werner still insisted that her boys be given a Hebrew education. Herb Werner learned Hebrew at the back of Mr. Madenburg's store. Madenburg was the only rabbi in the community for a while and the only one who could teach Hebrew. He, too, was poor, and owned only two chairs. Herb and his brother Sam took turns sitting while they learned their lessons. They also were interrupted constantly as their teacher waited on trade that came into the store during lesson time.

Herb Werner's Bar Mitzvah was held at Max Friedwald's house. Sam was the only one of the Werner brothers to receive an advanced education. He graduated from the University of Wisconsin, and then from Rush Medical School of the University of Chicago in 1935. He married Jeanette Cheyney Bernstein in Chicago in 1930, and it was her zeal and hard work that financed his education as a doctor of medicine. After interning in Wauwautosa, Wisconsin, and working for the government in Hayward, Wisconsin, from 1936 to 1938, Sam returned to Billings and his office was in the Hart Albin building in the 1950s. He and Jeanette adopted two children: Faith Abby and Nathaniel. The great tragedy of their lives was Nathaniel's death from cancer when he was seven years old. Sam Werner died prematurely from cancer in 1962, at the age of fifty-three, and Jeanette, heartbroken by the two losses, eventually moved back to Chicago.

By the 1950s, the only other Werners in Billings were Herb Werner, his wife Ruth, and their children Artie (Arthur) and Sara. Herb was in the insurance business, and the two children were among the "baby boomers" filling the religious school. They moved from Billings when the children had graduated from high school. Pete and Vera Werner lived in Livingston, Montana, where they built and operated the largest motel in town, and Pete's brother Maurice was in Napa, California. Peter was later in Montabello, California, and Israel Werner moved to San Francisco.

Max Friedwald was born in 1865 in Poland, but he grew up in Berlin. He remembered the anti-Semitism of the Germans and had an undying hatred for anything German. When he emigrated to the United States, he travelled to Deadwood, South Dakota, where he operated a saloon. He soon moved on to Billings and went into the same business.

Despite a limited formal education, Friedwald read widely and collected a library of Jewish-related books. He was considered the scholar of the community, and later willed many of his books to the Temple library. As he became more and more immersed in reading, he paid less attention to his business. His wife Fannie became responsible for running the saloon, which was a rough-and-tumble one. She perservered, however, and when Max died, the trustees of his estate, Louis Harron and Louis Melnick, discovered there was enough to support the widow and send $40,000 to the United Jewish Appeal.

In addition to the saloon, the Friedwalds had a second-hand store on Montana Avenue. Hyme and Frieda Lipsker lived in one of the apartments above the store when they were first married, and the Lipsker wedding took place in the Friedwald home, which hosted a number of important Jewish life cycle events.

Fannie Friedwald lived until March 23, 1959, and Rabbi Horowitz officiated at her funeral. The pall bearers were Sam Cohn, Leo Sigman, Morris Lipsker, Sam Melnick, Herbert Werner, and Jake Letwak.

Old-timers remember Dave Kohn. Kohn was a veteran of the Spanish American War who, after he was mustered out, went to work in the Butte mines. He married a Butte widow who had two sons, and the couple had twin sons of their own. After Dave's first wife died, he married Rose, and they had one son, Stanley Kohn. Kohn moved to Billings where he and his stepson Gershon provided one of the scandals that crept into local history when they had a shooting match over a business disagreement. Fortunately, no one was killed.

The Alfred Wagner family was very active in the Jewish community, and Alfred Wagner and Louis Harron were often the ramrods who kept B'nai B'rith together. Alfred traveled from Austria to Chicago to visit an uncle when he was fourteen years old. In a few years, he moved to Denver where he met and married his American-born wife, Jeanette. The couple also lived in Boise, Idaho, for a while, then decided they might do better in Miles City, Montana.

In Miles City, Alfred worked in a clothing store and Jeanette kept house and cared for their daughter Bernice. Soon their daughter Phyllis and son Jerome were born. With a growing family to support, Alfred decided it was time to strike out on his own. With five hundred dollars in cash, he opened a store in Broadview, Montana. Credit enabled him to expand the store. By the end of World War I, he decided to make the big move to Billings, where the youngest Wagner daughter, Marian, was born. Wagner opened a clothing store on Montana Avenue near the railroad depot. The store was later moved to the corner of Montana and North 27th streets, where it was run for a number of years by Bernice's husband, Wayne Braziel.

Bernice Wagner Braziel remembered the long hours her father worked, keeping the store open until at least eight each evening and much later on Saturday nights. Wagner's only recreation came on the weekends when there would be all-night poker games with Hyme Lipsker, Sam Letwak, and Dave Kohn. Bernice also remembered the fights among the clothing merchants—not friendly rivalry, but deep fear of competition. Petty problems aggravated the volatile situation. Hyme Lipsker owned the building housing Wagner's store, and periodically Lipsker got mad enough to threaten eviction.

By 1994, the only remaining Wagners in Billings are Marian Meyer and one of her sons, Richard Meyer, who followed Marian in the hair salon business.

In 1960, Max Bikman celebrated his seventy-fifth birthday and fifty years in Billings. Max came from a family of furriers in the Ukraine and was apprenticed to a tailor at the age of ten. Within two years he had mastered the details of tailoring and joined another tailor as a "full cloth mechanic."

An older brother who had emigrated to Baltimore, Maryland, invited young Max to visit his new country. While in Baltimore, Max remembered that a cousin had moved to Minneapolis, and tried to contact him. The answer came from Billings, Montana, instead. In the letter was a train ticket and an invitation to visit. Bikman related how, when the train arrived at the Billings railroad depot, his first sight was of dusty cowmen, blanket-clad Indians, and a sprinkling of townspeople. Beginning his two-week visit, he vowed to himself that as soon as the two weeks were over he would return to his native Ukraine. Bikman was unimpressed with the Billings area, but, he thought, as long as he was here, he would join his cousin in the tailoring work in the basement of a building at Minnesota and 27th Streets. He stayed longer than two weeks. After a year, he sent for a younger brother to replace him, and Bikman moved to another shop operated by Harry Truscott. Two and a half years later, Bikman moved again, this time to Canada, but after four years, he moved back to Montana, settling in Havre for six years.

Bikman also worked in Chicago and Sacramento, but he was continually drawn back to Billings. He worked as a tailor well past the age of seventy-five. His wife, Tillie Bikman, died in 1975; Max Bikman died in 1977. Both are buried in Beth Aaron cemetery.

The Letwaks have been in Billings since 1915. Their father came from Russia in 1915, landing in New York then going on to Milwaukee, Wisconsin, then Omaha, Nebraska, and finally arriving in Billings. Yetta Letwak was born first, in Omaha, and followed by her brother Jake Letwak. The Letwak family moved to Lovell, Wyoming, where they were in the hide business. Sam Letwak joined the Billings B'nai B'rith lodge as one of its out-of-town members, then finally decided to move to Billings. Yetta received her education in Billings and graduated from Billings High School in 1928. She then went to business college in Milwaukee, and by 1933, she had met and married Morris Niss, credit manager of a store there. The couple decided to move to Billings, looking for business opportunities in the midst of the depression.

At that time, all of the more established Billings hide buyers stopped working each year in the middle of June, since hides and furs were seasonal and since they worked hard during the winter months. Customarily Alfred Wagner, Sam Letwak, Hyme Lipsker, and Harry Goldberg would go to Cody to bathe in mineral springs, play cards, and relax. While the old-timers were out of town, young Jake Letwak and his new brother-in-law Morris Niss took the opportunity to survey the junk field. They wandered around the countryside gathering trailerloads of stuff. But when they returned to Billings, they could not get into the Letwak warehouse to unload their cache. Louis Harron came to their rescue and unlocked the warehouse for them. The long relationship and partnership between Jake Letwak and Morris Niss had begun.

Their next big deal occurred when they were on their way to Lovell. A big oil truck ran into four hundred sheep, killing all of them. The boys quickly bought all of the hides with a draft book, then hurried back to borrow money to cover the draft! The hides were sold to Sam Letwak, and the two young men found themselves with seven hundred dollars in profit.

During 1933 and 1934, Sam Vinner, a man named Holmes, and Sam Letwak were partners, with Jake Letwak as the junior partner. They barely scratched out a living, so they decided to sell and dissolve the partnership. The senior partners got four thousand dollars each, and Jake got fifteen hundred. Then Sam formed a new partnership with his son and son-in-law.

Morris Niss recalled during an interview:

> *Hides, you bought 'em and cured 'em and sold 'em. We bought hides from the ranches by contracting for them. In those days there were lots of losses. They were constantly dying. We would go into all*

the ranches in the area that had cattle and sheep. We would go from Billings to the Hi-Line and down into Wyoming to Casper. In 1933, a cheap hide was thirty cents, and they went as high as three dollars later on.

We would sell them by the carloads. Sometimes you would get twenty-five cents back: sometimes you would make money. There was no set price. If we got the hides green, we would salt them. If they laid in the salt too long, we had to take them out or re-salt them. We used the basement of the warehouse and laid them on the floor in a salt pack. It would take about two months. Such evil smelling stuff! Then we would shake the salt off, trim 'em (tails and snouts and ears), and find the different grades. If they weren't skinned right and were scored, they went for less money.

The Niss-Letwak partnership had ten thousand dollars to start with, and before long, they owed the bank $64,000. Morrie and Jake each drew fifteen dollars a week to live on, and Sam Letwak drew twenty. The men who worked for them got thirty dollars a week. Since their business needed a large amount of capital, they kept borrowing from the bank, and interest rates were high, usually eight percent.

Louis Melnick in Billings, Montana, 1914.
COURTESY OF SAM MELNICK.

"I remember the last time we went into the bank," said Morrie, recalling business in the Great Depression years. "We owed them about $49,000, but we told them we had to have more money or there was no business. Warren Vaughn's father said, 'What do you want? The bank?' 'No,' we said. 'We want $15,000.' We figured prices couldn't go any lower, and we had to keep buying hides. We got the money, kept selling things, losing money, putting money in the bank in the morning, and borrowing it in the afternoon. By 1939, things had picked up and we were making a fair living."

Sam Letwak decided to go to Europe to see his family in 1939, since things were looking grim over there and he was worried. While he was gone, Niss and Jake Letwak sold everything and went out of the hide and junk business. They became partners in the Billings Pipe and Supply Company, which they operated until 1965.

Jake Letwak married Frieda Bloom of Glendive, Montana. The Nisses and the Letwaks were long-time, staunch supporters of Congregation Beth Aaron. Frieda played the piano on Friday night for the services, and Jake was the self-appointed caretaker of the building.

Morris Niss died in Billings on December 10, 1973, and is buried in Beth Aaron cemetery. Now in their eighties, Frieda and Jake Letwak and Yetta Niss still live in Billings. None of their children stayed in Billings after high school.

Louis Melnick was secretary-treasurer of the Billings B'nai B'rith lodge for forty-five years. Melnick was born on November 4, 1892, in Greensberg, Pennsylvania; later he lived in Chicago, Illinois, where he had a little store. With the little stock he could bring with him, he moved to Billings in August 1913; within six years he had moved into the loan business, from there moving also into insurance. Once in Montana, he started a partnership with Harry Siegele; judging from the news in the *Billings Gazette*, it was not always smooth sailing. On February 25, 1914, the paper printed, "The partnership existing between Harry Siegele and Louis Melnick, proprietors of the Hoffman Store, 2505 Montana Avenue, was dissolved yesterday. Mr. Siegele is retiring and the business will be continued by his former partner." The situation had reversed a month later, since on March 24, 1914, the news read, "A co-partnership agreement filed yesterday by

"*Bragg on Melnick: One look at Billings and he stayed 65 years,*" February 1, 1979. COURTESY OF THE BILLINGS GAZETTE.

Annie, Sarah, and Abe Bookman. Courtesy of
the Sigman family.

Harry Siegele and Louis Melnick announces their intention of continuing the business of their Hoffman Store under the firm name of Siegele and Melnick. The agreement is for three years." But by 1922 Siegele was looking for something else, and he bought the Popular Store from Hyme Lipsker; he soon sold it back. Siegele then went back East, and after a series of business disasters and a brush with the law, he took his own life.

Melnick's big love was the Beth Aaron congregation, which he helped nourish. He served as its secretary-treasurer for fifty-five years, jealously guarded its treasury, and watched all expenditures. He never missed a congregation meeting because he wanted "to keep a handle" on decisions, particularly when it came to money.

Ada Cohen Melnick, Lou's wife, was born in Chicago, November 14, 1892, and married to Lou in 1914. She died in Billings at the age of sixty-seven. The couple had two sons, Sam and Charles. Charles Melnick moved to California early and seldom returned to Billings. Sam Melnick, a World War II pilot, came back to Billings after the war and became his father's partner. He met his first wife, Sue Rousso, while he was on duty with the U. S. Air Force in Montgomery, Alabama, and it was because of Sue's sister visiting Billings that Leo Sigman met and married his wife Rosa. The Melnicks were later divorced. Sam Melnick and his second wife Helen still reside in Billings in 1994. They host the annual Louis Harron Night at Beth Aaron, and can always be counted on to contribute to the life of the Jewish community.

Sam's only son, Steve Melnick, graduated from the U. S. Air Force Academy and lost his life in Vietnam. His daughters, all educated out of state, settled in other parts of the country.

Two generations of Sigmans were active in the Billings community. The Sigman family came to Montana from Russia during the homestead boom, between 1900 and 1918. Some of them had lived in Ireland after leaving Russia. A network of siblings, cousins and in-laws came to Montana to establish homes and businesses; at one time the families of Sigman-Kramer and Bookman-Buchman spread from Forsyth to Ingomar, Vananda, Sumatra, Jordon, Wason Flats, Benzein, and Billings. Most of them spoke English and Yiddish, all with an Irish brogue.

Abraham Bookman and his brother-in-law Simon Sigman were the first of the family to arrive in Montana. Abe's father, Rabbi Mayer Bookman, had emigrated to Ireland with his three sons and had become a prison chaplain in Dublin. Si's father and mother, Muta and Tobie Sigman, emigrated to Ireland in 1881 with his two sons and daughters and operated a dairy farm. Abe Bookman married Annie Sigman, Si's sister, on March 10, 1906.

Abe Bookman and Si Sigman sailed from Queenstown, Ireland, and arrived in New York City on December 23, 1906. They continued westward to Hettinger, North Dakota, where they lived in a sod hut and opened a general store in a tent. A year later they came to Melstone, Montana, to visit Charles Goldstein and his family, and in 1907 they

moved to Ingomar, Montana, where they opened a general store. Annie, Abe's young wife, soon joined them.

Ingomar had a large sheep-shearing operation; its post office opened August 12, 1910, with Si Sigman as its first postmaster. Sigman served in that post for almost three years. Naturally, when Bookman's niece Celia Chetkin (Rachel Bookman Chetkin's daughter) came for a visit, she met Si; they were married on September 19, 1914, in Helena, Montana. The newlyweds moved to Vananda, a small settlement twenty-three miles southeast of Ingomar, and opened a store. Celia's sister, Mae Chetkin, came in 1915 to live with the family and work in the Sigman store, the Vananda

Mae Chetkin.
COURTESY OF THE SIGMAN FAMILY.

Si Sigman and an oil-drilling machine, 1917, Vananda, Montana. COURTESY OF THE SIGMAN FAMILY.

Mercantile. The Vananda post office opened in 1912, and Si was again appointed postmaster, on March 12, 1920. He served as such until January 17, 1925.

The Vananda Mercantile was a large building of about twelve thousand square feet plus a shed for implements and storage. At one time, there were eight employees who sold everything from groceries to hardware to clothing to farm implements. In addition to being postmaster, Sigman was on the school board, sold hail insurance to the farmers, and bought hides and furs from trappers and ranchers. The store became the unofficial political center of the community.

Over the next few years many relatives came and worked in the Vananda store or established their own businesses in surrounding small towns. During the 1920s dust bowl years, most of the Sigman and Bookman families moved west, although several kept their homestead acreage. Abraham and Annie Bookman sold their house in Ingomar in 1920 and moved to Seattle, but within a few years they were back in Ingomar where they built a new home and store. When Abe died July 6, 1941, he was buried in the Beth Aaron Cemetery in Billings. The Bookmans had no children.

Si Sigman developed from a young immigrant boy from Dublin into one of the major builders of Vananda. At first, he and Celia lived in rooms in back of their store, but they built a three-bedroom house prior to the birth of their first child, Helen. Since there were few doctors in the area, Helen Sigman was born in Ingomar at the Bookmans' home. Simon and Celia's son Leo Sigman was born three years later, in 1917. Both children attended school in Vananda and graduated from high school in Forsyth.

Leo Sigman recalled that life in Ingomar was lively when economic

The Jersey Lilly Bar and Cafe, Ingomar, Montana. COURTESY OF THE SIGMAN FAMILY.

conditions were good, but from 1917 to 1935 things went steadily downhill. When the Sigmans finally decided to pack up and move, they had very little money but a ledger book of accounts receivable from farmers who were broke. The family moved to Billings, where Si went to work in a used furniture store owned by Max Friedwald. Years later, Celia recalled how, in order to get fresh water in Ingomar, they had to bring it in by barrels from Forsyth on the railroad. It was a pleasure to be in Billings with water from the tap. Leo recalled times when Louis Harron would come to Ingomar in his flivver to visit them and spend the night at their home. As soon as Si and Celia moved to Billings, Harron got Sigman to join the B'nai B'rith Lodge. He was inducted on January 8, 1936.

Sigman eventually purchased the store and operated it for several years as the Billings Mercantile. Documents found in a safe-deposit box in 1993, after Leo's death, indicate that on September 20, 1935, Max Friedwald and Simon Sigman entered into an agreement concerning the Billings Mercantile Company. Friedwald would keep sixty percent of the stock and Sigman would get forty percent. The store was to deal in new and used furniture. Sigman put up fifteen hundred dollars and a promissory note for his share. The interest charged was eight percent. Sigman would act as manager and also draw a weekly salary, in addition to his share of the profits.

Leo Sigman attended Rocky Mountain College for one year, then at-

SIGMAN'S 1935

Way back in 1935, when Billings was a lusty infant of 50 years Simon Sigman opened his store to serve the people of the Midland Empire with home furnishings. The store was located at 17 N. 26th Street. Prices, quality and service were RIGHT, and the business flourished.

SIGMAN'S 1940

In 1940, Leo Sigman joined his father in the firm. The same principles of price, quality and service met Midland Empire approval and the business expanded.

SIGMAN'S 1949

In 1949, Leo Sigman moved to the present location occupying half of the present building. Lines of furniture and carpeting were enlarged, customer services were increased, but the same principles of doing business were retained. So was the good will and PATRONAGE of the Midland Empire.

SIGMAN'S 1960

After a brief leave from the Billings business scene, SIGMAN FURNITURE returned in July of this year—now occupying 20,000 sq. ft. of selling floor and thousands of dollars in "wanted" home furnishings. Price, quality and customer service—principles of Sigman's through the years—have rapidly reestablished Sigman's as the Midland Empire's home furnishing headquarters. Sigman's appreciate the confidence that YOU—the people of the Midland Empire have shown—and will do our best to merit your continued support.

Bigger and Better Than Ever!
29th STREET AT MINNESOTA

Advertisement for Sigman's Furniture, 1960, as it appeared in the Billings Gazette.
COURTESY OF THE AUTHOR.

tended and graduated from the University of Montana and joined his father in the firm in 1940. Service in the 53rd Medical Department in the Pacific during World War II took him away from Billings, but he returned after the war and continued the tradition of Sigman's Furniture Store after his father's death at the age of sixty in 1946. Simon Sigman was buried next to Abe Bookman, with whom he had traveled from Ireland forty years earlier. Celia Sigman lived to age eighty-six and died in 1979.

In 1948 Rosa Rousso came to Billings to visit her sister Sue Melnick. She soon met Leo Sigman; they married. Their son Richard Simon was born July 28, 1949, daughter Marilyn following on October 15, 1951, and Michael Alan coming after on February 2, 1957. Leo and Rosa Sigman closed their store briefly in the late 1950s and moved to Spokane to operate a furniture business, but by July of 1960 they were back in Billings to open a large furniture store at 29th Street and Minnesota Avenue. For the next twenty-five years, Sigman's was the place people went to buy good furniture. Leo was dedicated to his business and to his customers. He was an active member of the community.

Sigman's Furniture Store was enlarged several times, and even after a bout of serious surgery and retirement, Leo could not resist the idea of being in the furniture business. He opened a smaller store and manned it until ill health forced another retirement. For many years Rosa worked in the store helping him. Leo Sigman died in 1993; Rosa still lives in Billings in 1994.

Richard Sigman works in the Washington, D.C., area. For years, Marilyn Sigman lived in Alaska where she was a biologist; in 1994 she moved to Oregon. Michael Sigman came back to Billings and worked with his father in the store. He married Linda Collison of Wisconsin, and their son Eric Michael was born in Billings in 1987. For a brief time, Eric represented the fourth generation of Sigmans to live in Billings, but Michael changed careers, and he and his wife decided to move back to the Midwest.

Sam Vinner, another of Billings's first Jewish residents, came to Montana from the Russia-Manchuria border in 1899. His family, which was in the tannery business, was considered wealthy; Vinner's sister was sent to France for her education, and Sam was sent to England. An uncle who had no children of his own took care of Vinner there, and planned a book education for him. But Vinner wanted to learn a trade instead, so he was apprenticed to a jeweler and learned jewelry-making. He spent six years in London as a jeweler's apprentice.

Although for a time Vinner believed he would spend the rest of his life in England, wanderlust set in. On a trip to New York, he decided that he really wanted to live in the United States. Because he wanted to see the entire country, he set off on a five-day, cross-country train trip to San Francisco, California. He liked the West Coast city so much, he wanted to settle there—until the big earthquake hit, just after his arrival. Vinner spotted an newspaper advertisement for a Butte, Montana, company that needed a jeweler, so he packed his bags and took off for Montana.

Vinner arrived in Butte on May 1, 1899, and to his horror found two feet of snow on the ground. Dressed in light clothes from California, he quickly decided that it was not the place to live. He did not even leave the train depot, but sat down to wait for the next train east. As he waited, he was approached by a friendly stranger who had witnessed his reaction to Butte. The man was a member of the Billings Commercial Club, which had deputized all of its members as good will ambassadors for Billings. The stranger did such a good job of selling the merits of the Magic City that Vinner decided to take a look. Sunshine and people sitting outside the Parmly Billings Library greeted Vinner, who decided that Billings was indeed a good place. He later said that though he had traveled with his father from Russia to Hong Kong, Japan, and London, he never had experienced the friendliness and seen the signs of prosperity that he initially found in Billings.

Vinner looked over the town's jewelry situation and found a store on the corner of Montana Avenue and 27th Street. He was offered a job there, but found no tools available for the hand-crafted types of jewelry he could make. He asked for a two-week trial nonetheless,

The old Parmly Billings Library (now the Western Heritage Center), Billings. COURTESY OF THE AUTHOR.

Securities Building, Billings, Montana. COURTESY OF LEO SIGMAN FAMILY.

and asked his prospective employer to give him the profit his work brought instead of a salary. Soon after, at a weekend auction in a crowded store, Sam heard a voice calling to him: "Sam Vinner, what in heaven are you doing here?" It was a jeweler named Bowman that Vinner knew from San Francisco. He had become an auctioneer, and was handling the proceedings for the evening. His enthusiasm for Vinner's work launched Sam's career and built his reputation.

At that time in Billings, women wore many lockets, lavalieres, and brooches; Vinner made all of these things. He and his employer worked out a sixty-forty split, and by 1910 had gathered all the equipment they needed and more business than they could handle. Vinner decided to go into business for himself, buying the gem stones from his former employer. For a brief time, LeRoy Greene (later a noted Montana artist) worked for Vinner as a jewelry designer. Vinner's entrepreneurial spirit drove him to mount a sales effort. He worked his way to Portland, selling his jewelry, then discovered that he had more orders than he could handle. Since his handmade merchandise took time to make, he hurried back to Billings.

As early as 1916, Sam began to have stomach and back trouble. The physical requirements of the jeweler's trade—constant sitting on a stool, leaning over close work—took its toll. A doctor told Sam to get out and do hard physical exercise to build up his abdominal muscles, or risk becoming an invalid. This he did.

In 1912, Vinner married a woman who had come to Montana from

Poland in 1905. Blanche Vinner bore one son, Jack. But sadly, within a few years, she was stricken with multiple sclerosis and was bedridden for the next thirty-seven years. Blanche wanted to become an American citizen, but could not leave her bed to go to court. On June 13, 1956, special permission was given to move the court to her bedside for a special naturalization ceremony. She died shortly thereafter.

After Blanche's death, Vinner married the woman who had cared for her for many years. Sophie Vinner remained a part of the Billings congregation after Vinner died in 1970.

George Sukin came to Billings in the 1920s. Born in Novorvdavsk, Poland, George moved to Palestine as a teenager. He joined a fighting group there but, as one by one his friends were killed in local fighting, he decided to leave the country. He got a job working on a steamship; after making several crossings, he had earned enough to emigrate to the United States.

A few months of work in the garment industry in New York convinced Sukin to look for other opportunities, and though he knew nothing about photography, he talked his way into a job with the Barnum and Bailey Circus as their circus photographer. When the circus arrived in Billings, Sukin decided it might be a good place to settle. He met Sam Vinner, and the two men teamed up to buy hides. Vinner found Sukin a place to live with an Orthodox Jewish family with three single daughters. Soon Sukin was married to one of them, Lillian. Sadly, she unfortunately died in childbirth, leaving an infant son.

George Sukin joined the B'nai B'rith lodge in 1925 when he was twenty years old. Since he had soon developed a dislike for the hide business, he opened a small clothing store called the Boston Store. A thriving trade developed with the American Indians who frequented the area, and the store became profitable. On one occasion, Sukin decided to travel east to buy goods for the store. Sam Vinner suggested that he go to Philadelphia and meet a family he knew who had single daughters—friend Sam was bound and determined to get the widower married again. He was successful, for George Sukin met his wife Goldie there, and they became parents of two boys, Jack and Robert.

Robert Sukin recalled sleeping on a chair Saturday nights while his father played pinochle with some of the other Jewish store owners after they closed their shops. Although they were bitter business rivals, they clung to each other socially. Sukin also remembers Louis Harron picking up the family in his Packard and taking them to religious services because Sukin had a car, but no tires.

By 1950 George Sukin realized that investing in real estate could be profitable. With financial help from friend Alberta Bair, the wealthy daughter of a successful sheepman, he bought his first building, on North Broadway and Third Avenue. He and Goldie ran a gift shop in the corner of the main floor of the building. They sold the store by the mid-1950s, and George invested in more real estate. He built a building on North 29th Street; when his sons finished college, they came back to Billings and operated a large clothing and sporting goods store there, next to the original Young Men's Christian Association building.

More stores and real estate kept father and sons busy for the next couple of decades. Always a believer in education, George Sukin studied the stock market and began investing for the education of future grandchildren. He also taught his own children the value of saving and investing, lessons that are still quoted well after his death. His daughter-in-law Sandy (Bob Sukin's wife) was particularly devoted to her father-in-law and took all of his advice to heart and repeated it often.

Both Jack and Bob Sukin married Denver girls, sorority sisters at the University of Colorado. Jack's wife Adrea and Bob's wife Sandra both were raised in traditional Jewish homes, and the Sukins became the first Jewish couples in Billings to keep totally Kosher homes. Meat was shipped in from Denver, dishes were changed at Passover, and all of the holidays were celebrated traditionally. Each couple had four children. Jack's children were Craig, who became a doctor; Karen, who became a lawyer; Lisa, a lawyer; and Michele, a merchandiser. Bob's children were Craig, a doctor; Rhonda, a lawyer; Allan, a CPA; and Michael, a medical student. The Sukin children were educated at Dartmouth, Harvard, and Brown, in both undergraduate and graduate work. All eight settled away from Billings.

In 1994, there are no longer any retail businesses operated by Jack and Robert Sukin, but they are active in the real estate business. Their mother Goldie Sukin lives in a retirement home in Billings.

The *Billings Gazette* featured a story on February 12, 1980 about Max Fregger, who was celebrating his one-hundredth birthday in Peoria, Arizona. Born in Russia, Fregger lived under the czarist regime for twenty-two years. Forced into the

Russian army, he escaped by running and walking for hours through a forest, looking for the border of the country. He saw a well-guarded farmhouse, and decided to try and bluff the guard. He walked right by the guard, whistling as if he lived in the house. The bluff worked, and the Polish family living in the house later took him to the border where once again he had to run, this time into Germany.

Fregger had just enough money to pay for a ticket to America, so he arrived in this country broke. To his horror he discovered that each immigrant had to have at least twenty dollars in cash. An uncle who had already settled in the United States loaned him the money, so he was allowed to get off the boat.

Fregger wanted to obtain a college education, and he worked in a grocery store and studied pharmacy. When he graduated he moved west. He operated pharmacies in Reno, Nevada, for a while, then he moved to Billings, Montana. He retired in 1960 and moved to Arizona.

In 1931 Jerome Kohn, Sr., and his wife Frieda opened the Jerome Kohn Company, a wholesale tobacco and candy business in Billings. They had two children, Claire and Jerome, Jr.; when Jerome Kohn, Sr., died prematurely in 1938, his son Jerry took over the business, actively assisted by his mother. Although Jerry Kohn had a law degree, he did not practice law because of his involvement in the family business. When Jerry was called to service in World War II, his mother and wife Betty kept the business alive, selling tobacco, candy, and sundries. After the war, the business was reorganized as a partnership. Frieda Kohn took over the bookkeeping and office management. Vending machines were eventually added to the original business.

Both Betty and Jerry Kohn were active in community events. They participated in the local Red Cross, Community Chest, and cancer drives, and were active in the men's and women's B'nai B'rith groups. Kohn began a long and very active participation in the Optimist Club, which he continued even after his business was sold and he became an insurance man.

Although she was not a Jew, Betty Kohn was always active in the Beth Aaron congregation. For years she played piano as an accompanist for the children's choir. Betty and Jerry's three children, Leslie, Sandy, and Jay, all had Bar and Bat Mitzvahs, and the girls were also confirmed. Leslie Kohn stayed in Billings and is a teacher in 1994. Sandra Kohn moved away and practices law. Jay Kohn lives in Butte and is a television newsman.

In 1994 there is only one Jewish-owned retail store in downtown Billings, Jason's. It belongs to the Alweis family. Like others', their story starts elsewhere.

Jessie Nachman was born in London, England, in 1882 to a Russian-born family. Her father was a tailor, and she and her sisters helped in the shop. The girls emigrated to Butte, Montana, in the early 1900s, influenced by the Kenoffel family, who had lived nearby in London. Jessie Nachman was an excellent seamstress, and she earned her living as an "alteration lady." She was soon engaged to Sam Kenoffel, but he jilted her to marry another. Soon Joe Alweis appeared on the scene. A recent Austrian immigrant, Alweis had peddled his way across the United States with a pack on his back, walking all the way. He was a very tall man, and his descendants in Billings all inherited his height. Joe and Jessie were married in Butte, then moved to Stevensville, Montana, to open their first store—its counters were the packing boxes in which the merchandise arrived. Their home life was also rustic; their house had no bathroom, just an outhouse.

The Alweis's next move was to Lewistown, Montana, where Joe opened The Hub department store. His son Norman Alweis had been born in Butte in 1911; the other two sons, Lester (1912) and Paul (1915) were born in Lewistown. Lewistown was very small at the time, and everyone knew everyone else. A favorite town activity was baseball, and Norm, in particular, loved to play. Younger kids would tag along to watch the Lewistown team practice and play. Periodically the "House of David" ball team came to town to play the locals, and a good proportion of the town would come to watch. Norm Alweis would have loved to be a professional ball player, but his eyesight was very bad and prevented him not only from pursuing a sports career but from obtaining the education that his brothers had. Both Les and Paul Alweis attended the Wharton School of Business at the University of Pennsylvania.

Joe Alweis was a good businessman and taught his three boys the skills he had developed in selling clothing. He was responsible for giving several young men their start in business. He set Norm and Les up in business in Glasgow, Montana, and they opened a second store near the Fort Peck Dam. Joe also set his nephew Morris Feuer up in a store, in Havre.

Norm Alweis married Shirley Gruenberg of San Diego in 1935. Norm and Shirley moved to Billings and had a store, Jasons (J. Alweis & Sons), and in 1938 Norm became a member of the Billings B'nai B'rith lodge at age twenty-seven. Paul was called to service in World War II. At the war's end, he and his wife Barbara came to Billings to take over management of the store, and Norm and Shirley moved to Dallas and opened a store there. Paul and Barbara were on a vacation in Europe with Billings friends, the Rosettos, during the mid-1960s when the four were involved in a tragic auto accident. Both men lost their lives, and Barbara was left with a permanently mangled leg.

Les Alweis married Rosella Miller of Minneapolis in 1937. Les and Rosella moved from Lewistown to take over the management of the Billings store, and Barbara and her daughter soon left Billings. The Lester Alweis family immediately integrated into the Billings community at large. They knew the Jewish families because they had come for holiday services, but their friendship spread throughout the community. Their children, Elaine and Don Alweis, had both been born and raised in Lewistown. Elaine went on to graduate from Mills College in Oakland, California, and marry Joel Ziskind of Ohio. The wedding was in Billings, at Temple Beth Aaron, but the couple moved to California. Don attended the University of Denver and met his wife Ellen Cohen at school. Upon graduation, they moved to Dallas and worked with their uncle Norm for a couple of years. Their son Sheldon was born in Texas. After Paul's death, Don and Ellen returned to Billings and joined Les in the Jason's store, which had become the most exclusive men's store in the area. Don and Ellen had their second child, Jody, in Billings. When Sheldon married Kentucky-born Tracy and joined his father and grandfather in the store, the three generations of men might all be there to greet their customers, and occasionally, Sheldon's two little girls, providing four generations of Alweises in Billings.

The entire family became a familiar fixture at all Temple Beth Aaron services and activities. Both Ellen and Don Alweis held numerous board and committee positions in the congregation, with Ellen serving as president and Don often serving as treasurer. In 1994, Don Alweis is treasurer and Sheldon Alweis is on the Temple board of trustees. Ellen helped to create the Judaic Studies program at Eastern Montana College, and several of the resident rabbis taught classes at the college under the auspices of the program. She also served on the Billings School Board and as leader of the Growth Through Art program. Her mother and father, Milton and Ruth Cohen, moved from Ohio to be near their daughter and joined the Beth Aaron congregation. Ruth passed away in 1993 and is buried in the Beth Aaron cemetery. In 1994, Milt lives at West Park Village, the same complex that houses Goldie Sukin and Rosa Sigman. My mother,

Esther Levy of Chicago, spent the last six years of her life there, as well, and she and the Cohens developed a late-in-life friendship.

Because Billings primarily has a Jewish community of twentieth-century roots, it continues to thrive with the descendants of these and other Jewish pioneers who found golden opportunities in the Treasure State.

Epilogue

Temple Beth Aaron, Billings, 1993. COURTESY OF THE AUTHOR.

Judaism appears to be alive and growing in Montana despite the small numbers of Jews and the vast distances between our rural state's communities. With the resurgence of interest in Judaism, it is possible that our state's Jewish communities of frontier days may again see growing congregations.

As a resident of Billings for the past forty years, I have seen the Billings Jewish community change. As Helena and Butte lost Jewish populations because children went out of state for educations and did not return, so, too, did Billings lose its youngsters. What makes the growing congregation of today in Billings different is the changing economy of the Magic City and the people it has attracted over the years.

During the 1950s and 1960s, there were many Jewish-owned businesses in downtown Billings. They were successful, and several had branches in other parts of town. A person could walk from Montana Avenue (which borders the railroad tracks) up Broadway for about four blocks and pass Wagner's Clothing Store, Sigman's Furniture, Baron's Jewelry, Monarch Clothing (owned by the Gordons), Ed Feldman's Clothing Store, Reliable Tent and Awning (owned by the Nemers), Jason's (owned by the Alweises), Q's Sport Store (owned by the Lipskers), Sukin's, Carl's Shoes (managed by Jack Kleinrok), Morgan's Jewelers (owned by Bud Morgan), State Fur (owned by Ed Bernstein), and smaller businesses such as Max Bikman's tailor shop, all owned or managed by Jews. At the same time, there was one practicing lawyer who was Jewish, Art Meyer, a relative of the Butte Meyers. The town also counted two Jewish oil men, Mel Brown and Harry Anisgaard; two doctors, Dr. Sam Werner and Dr. Perry Berg; and two college professors, Dr. Harold "Shorty" Alterowitz and Dr. Aaron "Al" Small. But almost everyone else in the Beth Aaron congregation was a merchant or from a merchant family.

In the 1990s, the character of the congregation has changed. For the most part, Beth Aaron members are professionals, in many fields. Many have come to be part of the medical center that has mushroomed in Billings. Today, the Beth Aaron congregation boasts of its professional members: Israel-born Dr. Uri Barnea, director of the Billings Symphony; Dr. Stephen Kramer and his wife Marilyn, field director for Senator Max Baucus; retired Dr. Perry Berg, his wife Karen, and his daughter Randi who moved back from San Francisco after many years; Dr. David Myers and wife Nancy; Dr. Ron and Marcia Orman; Dr. Don and Carol Roberts; Dr. Bill Rosen and Kim Gillan; Dr. Brian and Tammy Schnitzer; Dr. Gregg Singer; Jeff and Dr. Melinda Sanders; Dr. Stuart and Estelle Rubin; Eastern Montana College professors Dr. Deb Schaffer, Rachel Schaffer, and Dr. Sally George Wright; Leonard and Hilde Kaufman; Diane Kersten; Cheryl and Norm Honeyman, a psychologist; Amira Harper; Judie Gage, a physical therapist in the school system; Michael Bugenstein; Rachel Burns (of Red Lodge); Robert and Cindy Cadoff; Wanda Walker and Lenny Duberstein; Jeff and Judy Feldman; Donna Healey, a journalist; Candace and Henry Krewer; and Marcia Selwyn.

The congregation counts its old timers with pride, too. Still in Billings in 1994 are Les and Rosella Alweis; Don and Ellen Alweis; Aaron Small and his daughter Margo Small Beal, who returned to Billings with her son

Nathan; Rose Berlant; Jack and Candy Bonawitz; Florence Bresky; Ruth and Maurice Holas (of Glendive); Frieda and Jake Letwak; Sam and Helen Melnick; Marian Wagner Meyers; Maury and Zella Nemer; Robert and Linda Nemer; Yetta Niss; Rosa Sigman; Goldie Sukin; Jack and Adrea Sukin; Robert and Sandy Sukin; and me, Julie Levy Brown Coleman.

Many other people have come and gone, but there seem always to be more on the way, keeping the congregation active and growing. Beth Aaron's numbers remain fairly constant, and conversion has been responsible for many new and energetic members in recent years. The converts have come not only as spouses of Jews but also as individuals who have become interested in the Jewish religion and have taken advantage of the rabbinical presence to study and convert, or as children of mixed marriages who were not brought up in the faith but have sought their roots and studied Judaism as adults. One memorable occasion was the *Bar Mitzvah* of Jack Bonawitz, who was teaching at Billings Senior High and who studied Hebrew as an adult. He is one of the mainstays of the current congregation services; he and Steve Kramer take charge of High Holy Day services year after year, to make sure that the services run smoothly and that people take part.

And, of course, there are many Jews in Billings who choose not to identify with the congregation. Reports from other parts of the state indicate this is a statewide (and perhaps nationwide) condition. One estimate of the number of Jews in Montana is five hundred, with another five hundred who have chosen not to identify themselves as Jews. Yet interest in Judaism has grown, and whenever classes have been taught at the colleges, the attendance has been good, and interest high. Friday night services in Billings often have non-Jewish visitors interested in learning about the customs and history of the religion.

Majco, a statewide Jewish organization, has provided a link between the Jews of various communities. This is a big change from the many years when there was little contact, especially between Billings and the western communities. There was no contact between the Baron de Hirsch B'nai B'rith lodge of Butte and the Billings B'nai B'rith lodge, for example, until Billy Meyer was elected second vice-president of the district lodge. When Meyer was elected, he and a delegation of Butte members made an official visit to Billings, leading to some joint picnics held at the halfway mark, Bozeman Hot Springs. Today, Majco holds a big gathering once a year, at alternating sites, so members can get to meet one another and study together.

News of Jews around the state travels between synagogues. The bulletin of Congregation Beth Aaron dated October, 1993, had the following notices about other congregations:

The Helena Congregation will celebrate Sukkot with a service and dessert potluck. Members of the Hebrew School will also build and decorate a sukkah.

Congregation B'nai Israel of Butte is celebrating the 90th anniversary of the Butte Temple this year. Note cards featuring a painting of the Temple on the front available at Shamrock Travel Company in Butte. Student Rabbi Scott Melzer will also be returning for another year of leading services.

Congregation Beth Shalom, the greater Yellowstone Jewish Community centered in Bozeman, will be celebrating an outdoor Sukkot service. Members have organized a Tzedekah Committee and are working on plans for a religion education program for the year. Member Stanley Rosenberg has completed Rabbinic Aid studies.

Congregation Aitz Chaim of Great Falls has a new student rabbi, Dan Feder. Their Religious School schedule is in place, and they are planning an October rummage sale. The Great Falls Youth Group also invites Jewish teenagers to join them for the weekend of February 25-27 to celebrate Purim and to get to know one another. Anyone who is interested can call Natalie Fisher at 434-2880 in the evenings.

The New Missoula Jewish Community is looking forward to visits during the year from Rabbi Einat Ramon from Israel. She is a non-congregational conservative rabbi.

The Flathead Valley Jewish Community, centered in Kalispell, will celebrate Sukkot by building a sukkah. Members have organized an introduction to Judaism Study Group and are working on plans for their Religious School for the year.

If the Montana Jews of the late 1800s had had access to traveling rabbis, organization and maintenance of their congregations might have been easier. Circuit-riding rabbis would, I am sure, have been welcome as circuit-riding Methodist preachers were. Rabbi Horowitz proved this late, in the mid-1970s, when he traveled the state when needed. In the scrapbooks of Beth Aaron are funeral programs from Butte when Horowitz travelled to conduct services there, because there was no religious leader.

Services such as Horowitz's would have been welcome in the previous century too, in places like Ingomar and Vananda and Klein.

Certainly, in the three major communities I examined, the Jewish people of Montana overcame many obstacles to create and maintain their religious affiliations. Montana has always attracted the adventuresome and independent-minded; the determination of these Jewish pioneers to succeed was an important factor in our state's development. The golden opportunities that Montana has traditionally offered, first to miners in the gold fields, then to merchants supplying the miners, and now to professionals working for people's health and education, have resulted in a unique environment. Much of the strength of the various groups now comes from the support of non-Jewish spouses. Education of children is another glue that holds some groups together.

The future looks bright in Big Sky Country.

REFERENCES

INTERVIEWS
Bernice Wagner Braziel, Billings.
Sam Cohn, Big Timber.
Dave Erhlich, Butte.
Frieda Fligelman, Helena.
Earle Genzberger, Butte.
Fisher Gordon, Butte.
Phil Judd, Butte.
Leo Kenoffel, Butte.
Bernice and Yetta Lissner, Helena.
Louis Melnick, Billings.
Sigmund Meyer, Butte.
Ruth Lipsker Moss, Billings.
Morris Niss, Billings.
Celia Sigman, Billings.
Dorothy Silverman, Helena.
Joseph Sklower, Helena.
Sam Vinner, Billings.
Renata Weil, Butte.
Herbert Werner, Billings.
Belle and Norman Winestine, Helena.

UNPUBLISHED MATERIALS
Kelson, Benjamin. "History of the Jews of Montana." Master's thesis, Montana State University, 1950.

Minutes of the United Hebrew Benevolent Association. On deposit with the Union Trust and Savings Bank, Helena, Montana.

NEWSPAPERS
Anaconda Standard
Billings Gazette
Butte Intermountain
Helena Herald

BOOKS

Campell, William C. *From the Quarries of Last Chance Gulch*, 2 vols. Butte: Ashton Printing & Engraving Co., 1951.

Davis, Jean. *Shallow Diggin's*. Caldwell, Idaho: The Caxton Printers, Ltd., 1962.

Golden, Harry. *Forgotten Pioneer*. Cleveland and New York: The World Publishing Company, 1963.

Hamilton, James McClellan. *From Wilderness to Statehood*. Portland: Binford & Mort, 1957.

Howard, Joseph Kinsey. *Montana: High, Wide, and Handsome*. New Haven: Yale University Press, 1959.

Langford, Nathaniel Pitt. *Vigilante Days and Ways*. Chicago and New York: A. L. Burt Company, 1890.

Leeson, M. A., ed. *History of Montana, 1739-1885*. Chicago: Warner, Beers, & Co., 1885.

McCracken, Harold. *The Charles M. Russell Book*. Garden City, N. J.: Doubleday & Co., Inc., 1957.

Miller, James Knox Polk. *The Road to Virginia City: The Diary of James Knox Polk Miller*. Edited by F. Rolle. Norman: University of Oklahoma Press, 1960.

Progressive Men of the State of Montana. Chicago: W. W. Bowen & Co., 1902.

Reymer, Robert George. *Montana, the Land and the People*. Chicago and New York: Lewis Publishing Co., 1930.

Rochlin, Harriet, and Fred Rochlin. *Pioneer Jews: A New Life in the Far West*. Boston: Houghton Mifflin Co., 1984.

Sanders, Helen Fitzgerald. *A History of Montana*. Vols. 1, 2, and 3. Chicago and New York: Lewis Publishing Co., 1913.

Sanders, James U. *Society of Montana Pioneers*. Vol. 1. Akron, Ohio: Werner Co., 1899.

Stout, Tom, ed. *Montana, Its Story and Biography*. Vols. 1 and 2. Chicago and New York: The American Historical Society, 1921.

Toole, K. Ross. *An Uncommon Land*. Norman, Okla.: University of Oklahoma Press, 1959.

Wolle, Muriel Sibell. *Montana Pay Dirt: A Guide to the Mining Camps of the Treasure State*. Denver: Sage Books, 1963.

INDEX

ABOUT THE AUTHOR

Julie Coleman. PHOTO BY CANDACE DURAND. COURTESY OF THE AUTHOR.

Julie L. Coleman was born and educated in Chicago, Illinois. She also attended the University of Wisconsin, Roosevelt University, and Eastern Montana College. She moved to Billings, Montana, in 1952, and developed an interest in the history of the Treasure State. Volunteer work as president of the League of Women Voters and state board membership in that group took her to the state capital, Helena, where she developed a network of personal contacts in the Montana Jewish community. Personal interviews and original source material amplify her research on the Jewish pioneers of Helena, Butte, and Billings.

A retired social studies teacher, she has been a stockbroker since 1980. She holds bachelor and master's degrees in education, and is currently first vice-president of investments in the Billings office of the national brokerage firm of Dean Witter Reynolds.